DAVID DUNFORD

Ensign
PUBLICATIONS

First published in 1994 by
Ensign Publications
2 Redcar Street,
Southampton SO1 5LL.

a b c d

Publisher David Graves.
Designed by Precinct Press.
Cover by Design Laboratory.
Photography by Richard Scott.
Maps by Jack Street.
Printed by Short Run Press, Exeter.

ISBN 1 85455 104 3

Cover: *The Blue Boar Inn*, Longworth (Walk 5)

Walk · CONTENTS · Page

· INTRODUCTION ·

Oxfordshire is not a county of dramatic scenery; it has no waterfalls, no sea cliffs nor mountains. However, although it could hardly be described as spectacular, the countryside is certainly not uninteresting. The attraction of the area is in its villages, its history and its gentle landscape of river, wood and hill. The most important geographical feature is the River Thames, which flows from west to east through the county collecting tributaries as it goes. Many of the walks in this book include a riverside section — as well as several beside the Thames itself, there are walks along the rivers Evenlode, Cherwell, Ock and Windrush, and along the towpath of the Oxford Canal.

The centre of the county, politically and physically, is the city of Oxford. A number of books could be written on walks in Oxford alone. I have included a few routes that pass close to the city centre — it is surprising how close one can get without being overwhelmed by tarmac, tourists and traffic. Outside Oxford itself are several attractive market towns (Abingdon and Witney are represented here) and dozens of pretty villages. Many of these settlements have had brushes with fame in the past—royal connections, important visitors, Civil War skirmishes and famous tombs all feature.

Oxfordshire seems to have more than its fair share of fine old inns — very few of the pubs featured in this book are less than 200 years old. Many of the walks pass two or more pubs, but you should not infer that those I mention in passing are any less welcoming or interesting than those I describe more fully. The pubs I have concentrated on are those that appealed to me, and which make convenient starting points or rest stops for the walks.

With a few exceptions, I have been surprised by the good condition of the footpaths as I have researched this book — very few of the dotted lines on the map are obstructed or invisible on the ground. I suspect that this would not have been true a few years ago. With more understanding between walkers and landowners, perhaps this welcome trend will continue. To this end, please respect the country-side and follow the Country Code.

DAVID DUNFORD
March 1994

Along the ridge from Fernham to Little Coxwell

WALK 1
Allow 2 hours
4 miles
Walk begins page 8

Background to the Walk

An outcrop of sandy Lower Greensand rock elevates this area above the surrounding Vale of White Horse, so the views are extensive (the same rock makes up the notable eminence of Faringdon Folly). A few tourists seek out the impressive Tithe Barn at Great Coxwell or climb to the Folly, but very few venture to find the peaceful and pretty villages of Fernham and Little Coxwell. Both villages have village pumps — the pump near Fernham church stands above a stone-lined bottle well (now capped); that at Little Coxwell is surrounded by sarsen stones. Fernham's name means simply 'the water meadow where ferns grow'. Its church is wholly Victorian and warrants a paltry three lines in the Berkshire volume of Nikolaus Pevsner's *The Buildings of England*, but the church at Little Coxwell has plenty of interest. Features visible from outside include the 13th-century twin bell turret with a sundial, and the 15th-century south porch which conceals a Norman doorway. If the church is unlocked, inside you will find a Norman nave with a narrow chancel arch, a 500-year-old font and a 15th-century gallery. The church was once owned by the abbots of Beaulieu in Hampshire; the abbot received a supply of mutton and wool from the Vale's sheep as part of the arrangement. The churchyard is carpeted with cowslips and primroses in spring.

Coles Pits are marked on the Ordnance Survey map to the right of the path as it climbs towards Galley Hill. This 14-acre site was once pock-marked with round depressions, some up to 22 feet deep and 40 feet wide, whose origin was something of a mystery. Various visitors have counted the pits and come up with totals

Maps
Landranger 1:50,000
Sheets 164 and 163
Pathfinder 1:25,000
Sheet 1135 (SU 29/39)
Map Reference of Start/
Finish SU292919

How to get there
From the A420 Faringdon bypass, take a turning to the south, signposted to Little Coxwell and Fernham. Pass the turning to Little Coxwell on the right, and the entrances of Ringdale Manor on the left and St. Mary's Priory on the right. When you reach a T-junction in Fernham, turn left, to find the Woodman Inn almost immediately on your right. Fernham village is served by two infrequent Regis Coaches services (tel. 0367 718929) from Faringdon and Wantage, and by the Swindon & District service 66 between Oxford, Faringdon and Swindon (tel. 0793 522243).

Pub facilities
Woodman Inn, Fernham
(Pictured right)
The Woodman is no ordinary village pub. It boasts a log fire, a banqueting hall and a collection of over 100 hats hanging behind the bar; smokers can sample a filled clay pipe (supplied by the only surviving British manufacturer). Unusual drinks are available, such as mead and country fruit wines. More conventional tastes will be satisfied by the choice of real ales. Theakston's Old Peculier and Morland's Original are regulars, and are supplemented by three or four guest beers. A good and changing selection of food might include beef and bitter cobbler or a choice of curries. Specials might be home-made steak and kidney pie, chilli con carne or Woodman hotpot. Vegetarians and vegans are well served, with at least 5 meat-free dishes such as brown bean chasseur, couscous with chickpea stew or fennel and pasta in tomato sauce. There is a small garden and car park. Children are welcome in the garden and the back room near the food bar. The pub is closed on Monday lunchtimes, and no food is served on Monday evenings. Otherwise, opening hours are from 1100 to 1500 and from 1800 to 2300 (with normal Sunday hours) and food is available from 1200 to 1400 and from 1930 to 2130. Tel. 0367 820643.

Eagle Tavern, Little Coxwell
Midway round the walk is the Eagle Tavern, run by Mark Lawrenson, the ex-Liverpool and Eire footballer, who also managed Oxford United.

ranging from 60 to 300. The name Coles Pits, recorded as early as 1687, suggests a link with Old King Cole of nursery rhyme fame (who was probably a genuine historical figure, a British prince who came to the throne in the 3rd century AD). The nearby village of Coleshill has also been linked with this shadowy ruler. Early antiquarians suggested that the pits were the remnants of an ancient British village of pit dwellings, perhaps housing as many as 1400 people. Modern archaeological thinking has it that the pits were dug for stone to make querns or grindstones, and a find of several pieces of broken millstone in the 1930s supports this view. Sadly, the site was bulldozed in the early 1960s.

The stone found in this area, which is still quarried near the Faringdon bypass, is highly fossiliferous. Some of it contains large numbers of marine sponges, and a yellow-orange gravel known as 'sponge gravel' was once in great demand for ornamental avenues and walks. Fossil sharks' teeth are also occasionally found, as are the palatal teeth of certain fossil fish. These were once thought to be stones from the heads of toads, and were credited with powerful medicinal properties. Some of the local stone has been identified in the walls of Calleva Atrebatum, the Roman town at Silchester near Reading.

Midway through the walk, there are extensive views to the north from Galley Hill. Galley Hill may be a corruption of Gallows Hill, and a very suitable place it

Little Coxwell church has a 13th-century bellcote

would have been for a gallows — on a commanding site always visible as a deterrent to any would-be villains in nearby Faringdon. Nowadays there is nothing more sinister than a lone tree. The view from the hill includes, in the extreme west, the hill-top village of Highworth in Wiltshire. To the right of this is the wooded Badbury Hill. The trees conceal a hillfort, said to be Mons Badonicus, site of a famous victory of King Arthur. To the right of the hill one can see into the valley of the upper Thames, then further east is the town of Faringdon with its Norman church tower prominent among the buildings. The aircraft of RAF Brize Norton, mostly Tristars and VC-10s, can usually be seen lined up on the runways directly behind the town and to the right is Faringdon Hill.

During the Civil War, Faringdon House was held by the Royalists until it was bombarded into surrender from Faringdon Hill by the Parliamentarians after the fall of Oxford. During the attack, the church spire was demolished. Oddly enough, the man responsible for the cannon-fire was Sir Robert Pye, the owner of the very house he was attacking! The tower that now stands on the hill was one of the last follies to be built in England. It was erected in 1935 to a design by the then Duke of Wellington, and is occasionally open to the public. Interestingly, the hill seems to have been known as Folly Hill even before the present tower was built. The Scots Pines around the tower were planted at the direction of Sir Henry Pye, MP for Berkshire, who owned Faringdon House in the 18th century. He was made Poet Laureate by William Pitt in 1780. Despite holding the post for 23 years, he does not seem to have been a particularly talented poet — his most enduring work is the nursery rhyme *Four and twenty blackbirds*, though he also wrote a long poem *Faringdon Hill* extolling the scenic virtues of his favourite viewpoint.

Not far from Coles Pits, on the heights above Little Coxwell, is Ringdale Manor. The remains of a hillfort, probably Iron Age in date, lie within the grounds, but little of the fort is now discernible. The circular fortifications may have been the inspiration for the manor's name. The house was built of Cotswold stone in the early part of the 20th century; some of the interior walls on the ground floor are lined with Jacobean panels from Beachampton Hall near Milton Keynes in

Buckinghamshire. The original Ringdale Manor, below the hill beyond the Little Coxwell road, is now St. Mary's Priory, a Benedictine convent.

Two possible excursions suggest themselves for car drivers before you turn for home. Firstly, the nearby tithe barn at Great Coxwell is an impressive sight and is usually open to the public — to reach Great Coxwell, return to the Faringdon bypass, then turn left and first right. Alternatively, a mildly exciting expedition is to drive the few miles from Fernham to the White Horse and negotiate the steep lane that passes just under the Horse. Park in the large car park on the downward leg (not the small car park at the top which is intended for the elderly and disabled) and stroll up to view the ancient White Horse at close quarters. Here you can also wander around the large hillfort of Uffington Castle and overlook Dragon Hill and the deep downland combe of The Manger. This is far and away the most impressive scenery in Oxfordshire.

Walk 1

Distance: *Allow about two hours for this easy walk with superb views.*
Note: Parts of this walk may be muddy in wet weather, and there is a steep descent at the end of the walk — walking shoes or boots are recommended. This is pheasant-rearing country, so please keep dogs on leads.

From the Woodman Inn walk right. When the road bends right, keep straight on along Chapel Lane. Ignore a footpath signposted between houses on the left (this is our return route), instead keeping on to the gates of Fernham House Farm. Here cross a stile on the left into a field which shows traces of ridge and furrow (relics of ancient strips of land ploughed by oxen). Keep along the bottom of the field with the farm buildings on your right to a field gate. Pass through this and aim slightly left to a second gate. Beyond, the path leads through a third field to a gate into a hedged and fenced track above South Farm House. Turn left.

This bridleway, used regularly by horses and a little muddy in places, leads gradually uphill. As it does, it gets firmer and sandier underfoot, and for most of its length is bordered by small copses and windbreaks (look out for Siskins high in the pines in winter). There are good views eastwards over the Vale towards Didcot Power Station on the right. When the path descends into a belt of sycamore woodland, a path departs on the right. Unless you want to take a look at the small reedy pond, or examine the old railway (a disused spur from the main Great Western Railway to Faringdon), follow the track straight on.

At the bottom of this dip, notice the thick bed of sand that has been washed from the surrounding hillsides. Leave the woodland and walk up a stony, sandy path in a slight dip in the hillside. At the top of the hill, where a footpath sign indicates another path to the left, admire the view then continue onward down the hill. This leads to a crossing of paths at the end of a quarry, close to the Faringdon bypass. Turn left, and follow a farm track past a barn and parallel to the bypass, with the steep slope of Galley Hill on the left. When you reach the road, turn right and walk along the road for a short distance. Just short of a mature oak tree on the right, turn

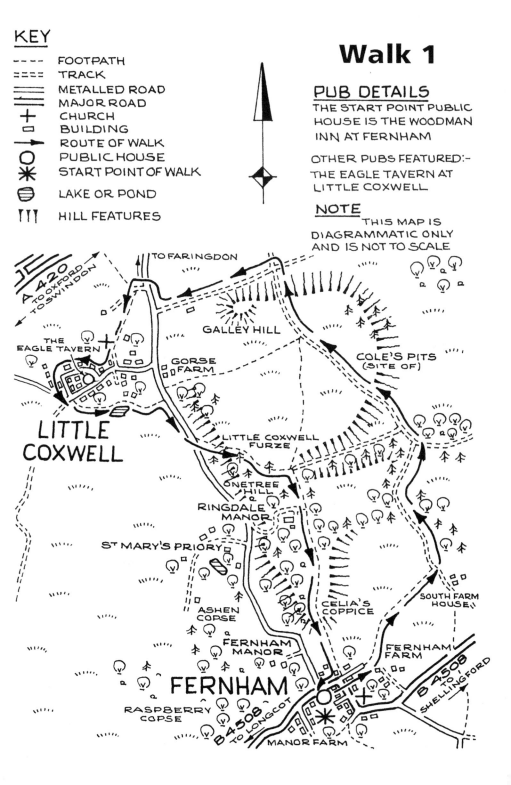

left along a footpath signposted to Little Coxwell. Almost immediately, cross a stile on the left which leads you into a fenced path across a field towards Church House, a fine Georgian house built of brick in around 1720. The path runs along the wall of this property, then leads to a gate into the churchyard of Little Coxwell.

Leave the churchyard by the lych-gate, then walk down the metalled path to the main village street. Follow this to the right past thatched cottages to the Eagle Tavern by the old village pump. Turn right and follow the lane past a fine creeper-covered house on the right and the Methodist Church on the left. The road bends left by a small triangular green, then meets another village street at a T-junction. Cross straight over, and turn left in front of a hay barn. Pass through a gate with some wooden stables on the left, and follow a path that runs behind the gardens (notice the superior playhouse which extends into the field with a bridge to one of the gardens). The wall on the left is a 'ha-ha' — a sunken wall designed to keep animals out of the garden without interrupting the view from the houses.

Cross a fence to the left of a line of cypresses, then walk between a wall and a tennis court to a duck pond which is usually graced by a pair of handsome Muscovy Ducks. Beyond the duck pond, follow the farm track through a gate, then skirt a second pond (probably an old quarry, to judge by the small rock face at its rear). Follow the hedge round to the left, then cross another gate. Walk along the edge of the paddock straight ahead to the road, where there is an old, rather high, stone stile.

Turn right along the road, then take a bridleway on the left which leads up a shallow dry valley to a wood. Follow the path up through the trees. This area is home to hundreds of pheasants — which may startle the unsuspecting walker when they rocket from the undergrowth! When the conifer plantation on the left ends and the track begins to drop, turn right. This path leads behind Ringdale Manor, with yet more good views to the left whenever there is a gap in the trees.

Beyond the Manor, the path begins to descend. As you leave the trees you encounter the most dramatic moment of the walk, when you are suddenly confronted with a wide view of the Vale of the White Horse, with the White Horse itself forming an impressive backdrop. The path starts to descend towards Fernham, passing Celia's Coppice at the end of the ridge. After a steep descent with a stile part way down, the path runs along the edge of a couple of fields. It then passes between gardens to return to Chapel Lane. Turn right and return to the Woodman.

A peaceful woodland walk from Buckland

WALK 2
Allow 3 ½ hours
6 ½ miles
Walk begins page 13

Background to the Walk

This figure-of-eight route crosses itself in the middle of Buckland Warren, giving the walker two opportunities to appreciate the peace and beauty of this woodland area. The Warren lies in an area of out-cropping sand, which is quarried nearby (a small active pit is passed midway round the route). Certain trees such as Scots Pine and Sweet Chestnut flourish in the sandy soil. The soil also has the advantage to walkers that it stays generally dry underfoot (except in a few places). The woodland hosts a variety of wildlife. Bird species often seen here include Goldcrest, Coal Tit and Long-tailed Tit; deer (mainly the pig-like Muntjac and native Roe) are glimpsed rather less often.

At the beginning or end of the walk, a visit to Buckland church is recommended, even to those who would not normally be interested in such places. It has several fascinating features — original 12th-century hinges and ironwork in the south door; an ancient iron-bound chest with a coin slot which, it has been suggested, may have been used to collect contributions for the Crusades; two 16th-century ceremonial helmets on the wall; a window dedicated to one William Niven, an ancestor of the actor David; and a stunning Victorian transept decorated with blue and gold mosaic and painted marble (designed by Henry Holiday, who illustrated Lewis Carroll's *The Hunting of the Snark*). Perhaps the most interesting feature is a triangular locker in the north wall of the chancel, near the altar. This contains a 'heart burial'. William Holcott was an outspoken Protestant preacher who recanted when Mary Queen of Scots came to the throne, but reverted

Maps
Landranger 1:50,000
Sheet 164
Pathfinder 1:25,000
Sheet 1135 (SU 29/39)
Map Reference of Start/
Finish SU342978

How to get there
From the A420 Oxford-Swindon road, take the Buckland turn 3 miles east of Faringdon. Follow Buckland Road past Summerside Road on the right, then look out for the concealed entrance to The Lamb Inn on the left opposite the entrance to Orchard Road. There is limited extra parking at Buckland church, 100 yards beyond the pub. The Oxford-Swindon service 66 (operated by Swindon & District buses) stops at Buckland Turn on the A420 (four journeys per day in each direction; no Sunday service).

Pub facilities
The Lamb at Buckland
(Pictured right)
The Lamb at Buckland is a former coach-house in a quiet lane off the main street. It has hotel and restaurant facilities, as well as the bar. Morland's Original, Old Speckled Hen and a guest beer are on offer, plus a range of lagers and soft drinks. Occasionally wine-tasting events are held here. The beams are draped with hops, and there is an open fire. The Lamb has a good reputation for food; the menu includes starters and snacks (eg.Welsh rarebit, grilled Cornish mackerel or ploughman's lunch with farmhouse cheeses), as well as more substantial dishes such as Dover sole, seafood risotto, roast grouse and saddle of venison. Food can be eaten in the bar or restaurant, on the patio or at tables in the large garden. Children are welcomed, as are dogs on leads. There is a large car park. Most credit cards are accepted. Accommodation (two doubles, two twin bedrooms, all en-suite) is available. Tel. 0367 87484.

The Lamb at Buckland

to Protestantism when Elizabeth I was crowned. He willed that his heart should be buried at Buckland, and his request was observed when he died in 1575; the rest of his body was interred in London. The handbook for visitors (on sale in the church) gives further details of all these curiosities and more.

There are two fine 18th-century country houses on the route. Buckland House, which is seen well as you approach the end of the walk, is attributed to John Wood the younger, who also designed the Royal Crescent at Bath. It was built for Sir Robert Throckmorton in 1757. His son, Sir John Throckmorton, once bet a thousand guineas that two of his sheep could be shorn and a hunting coat made from the wool between sunrise and sunset on the same day. A Newbury manufacturer accepted the challenge, and completed the coat in 13 hours and 20 minutes. Sir John wore it at dinner that evening. It hung in the house for many years, along with another interesting article of clothing — the chemise worn by Mary Queen of Scots at her execution at Fotheringay Castle, complete with bloodstains. The house became known as University Hall, Buckland, in 1963 when it opened as an educational charity to educate students otherwise unable to enter a university. The college provides courses of tuition for degrees from the University of London in Law, Economics and Management Studies. The old manor house can be seen behind the church — it was built in the 16th century, but was converted to 'Gothick' stables after the new house was built.

The second stately house is at Pusey. Probably its most famous inhabitant was Edward Bouverie Pusey, who was born here in 1800. Pusey was leader, with Keble and Newman, of the Oxford Movement, which aimed to restore 17th-century

High Church ideals to the Church of England. The Bouverie family adopted the name Pusey when they took over the estate, as had earlier tenants. The house is famous for its gardens which include an ornamental lake and Chinese bridge.

Buckland House, now home to University College, Buckland

Like Buckland, Pusey House once contained a famous artefact with royal associations. Pusey's was the Pusey Horn, which now re-sides in the Victoria and Albert Museum. This priceless relic is an ancient drinking horn with a 15th-century silver mount inscribed 'Kynge Knoud geve Wyllyam Pewse thys horne to holde by the londe'. The story behind the horn is as follows. Around the year 1015, King Canute (Cnut) was encamped at Cherbury Camp (an unusual hillfort on flat land between Pusey and Charney Bassett). William Pusey, one of Canute's officers, disguised himself as a shepherd and infiltrated the enemy camp at White Horse Hill and learnt of a plot to ambush the king. Canute was warned and thus avoided the ambush; in gratitude he gave the officer a horn and all the land within earshot when it was sounded. This method of tenure, known as 'cornage' or 'horngeld', was one of the oldest forms of title deed. There are only five such horns in the country.

A feature of this walk is two free-standing dovecotes visible from the path. The first, in a garden in Pusey, is late 18th century and made of brick; the second, at Home Farm on the edge of Buckland Warren, is in stone with 'vermiculated' bands at first floor and eaves level. Both are Grade II listed by the DoE.

Walk 2

Distance: *Allow between three and four hours for this walk of six-and-a-half miles through village, farmland and woodland.*

From The Lamb Inn, walk along the drive back to the main village street. Turn left and proceed to a T-junction. Cross straight over and follow a driveway as far as a gate. Here, turn right and pass in front of the church. Beyond the church, walk past a cottage with a metal plate dating it to 1820. When you reach a metalled lane in front of a pair of gateposts, admire the view over the Thames valley on the left, then turn right. When you regain the main village street, turn left. Follow the street round to the left, then to the right in front of a mature lime tree, which has given its name to the pretty thatched cottage on the left. Keep on round the bend and then walk slightly downhill passing a small wood on the left. When the road bends right for a second time with a footpath leading off to the left, take the footpath that leads straight on along the edge of a field to the A420.

Cross the main road carefully and cross a stile a few yards to the right over a fence into a field (there is a footpath sign to Pusey). Walk along the right-hand edge of this field, then turn left just before you reach the farm at the far end of the field. Cross a stile in the far corner of the field. Beyond this, the path follows a line of telegraph poles to another wooden stile (there is also a worn stone stile in the tumbledown dry-stone wall here). This leads into a narrow belt of woodland, which has been widened by recent planting. Beyond the wood, the track leads across a large field to a gate in Pusey village. Cross the gate into the road.

Turn right past some estate houses (one of which is quaintly named Peasinapod) by a small green with an old pump. A short way beyond the last house in the village, a bridleway is signposted to Faringdon on the right. Follow this between two fences, noting the dovecote in a garden on the right, to a belt of woodland. Beyond the wood, the path leads through a gate and onwards through crops. The last section of this path runs alongside the drive to the restored Broadmoor Cottage.

When you reach the Buckland-Gainfield road, cross straight over into a bridleway. This leads across a couple of fields, with woods on either side, until it reaches the shade of Buckland Warren. The path can be rather muddy by the stream just inside the wood, but it improves beyond as the path rises slightly. The path leads to a crossroads of paths; keep straight on here, to pass an area of newly planted conifers on the left. Notice the two Chilean Pine (Monkey Puzzle) trees on the right. Several tracks and rides cross at right angles. These are private and should not be followed, but do glance down each one; you may be lucky and see deer crossing from one block of trees to the next. Eventually, the path reaches the edge of the wood (with Faringdon Folly noticeable straight ahead). The path leads between two fences across a newly created (1992-3) golf course, then between two gates, through a gap in a hedge and straight across a large field.

When you reach a minor road, keep straight on (left). Ignore the bridleway straight on, instead following the road to the left around a house called The Hideaway. The route follows this quiet country lane for about a mile, with distant views to Uffington White Horse and beyond to the right. The towers of the churches at Hatford and Stanford-in-the-Vale are visible straight ahead. Partway along, there is a small sand quarry on the left. It is worth taking a look through the conifers at the quarried edge, which shows the bright reds and oranges of the sand. In some years a small colony of house martins has nested in holes in the cliff, but this is likely to be a short-lived phenomenon.

Beyond the quarry the route continues along the lane until you reach a group of barns on the left just short of Hatford village and opposite a house called The Woodlands. Take the bridleway to the left just beyond the barns, which leads

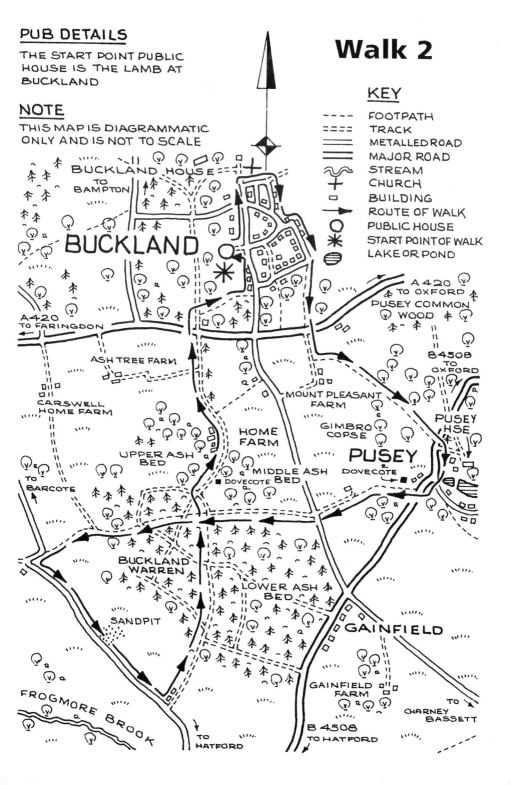

across a field back into Buckland Warren. At the edge of the wood, the path crosses a stream, then swings left. At the top of a rise, you cross a perpendicular track, then follow an intriguing section through a shadowy avenue of yew trees. Beyond this, the path develops into a grassy ride through coniferous woodland, where butterflies such as Speckled Woods and Red Admirals (and possibly rarer species such as Fritillaries) may be seen. At the end of this stretch, you cross the path you followed earlier. The path beyond joins a gravelly track and crosses a field. Cross the stream again, and pass the second dovecote. The path then skirts the buildings of Home Farm (notice the decorative window in the farm cottage which echoes the quatrefoil shape of the blind windows of the dovecote). This farm drive, now metalled and lined by Scots Pines, leads back to the A420.

Cross straight over to a gateway, and pass a small lodge. Beyond this, cross a stile to the right into a field. The woods between the main road and this field are thick with Snowdrops in early spring. Head half-right across the bottom of the field, with good views of Buckland House to the north, to a stile on the eastern side. This gives access to a pleasant stretch of path through a wood. This ends all too soon at a stumpy stone stile which leads out into the road in Buckland. Turn left and walk the short distance back to The Lamb Inn.

Chalk hills and cress beds from Letcombe Regis

WALK 3
Allow 2 hours
3 ¹/₂ miles
Walk begins page 20

Background to the Walk

The name of Letcombe Regis will probably ring a bell for followers of racing, for this is prime racehorse country. Captain Tim Forster has his stables at Letcombe Regis; successful horses trained here include *Well To Do, Ben Nevis* and *Last Suspect*, winners of the Grand National in 1972, 1980 and 1985 respectively. Lester Piggott, who has won the Derby no fewer than nine times, was born in Wantage Hospital in 1935 and lived in an unassuming red-brick house in Letcombe Regis until his family moved to Lambourn when he was eleven years old. Strings of racehorses can often be seen being led around the lanes.

Another local industry, for which Letcombe Regis and Letcombe Bassett were once famous, is the growing of watercress. 'Bassett cress!' was once a familiar street call in the markets of London. Watercress beds can still be seen where the road between the villages crosses Letcombe Brook. The industry suffered badly in the drought of 1976, but survived. Thomas Hardy used Letcombe Bassett (thinly disguised as Cresscombe) as a setting for a scene in *Jude the Obscure*, first published in 1895. Jude is musing on the classical authors he will study at Oxford as he walks through the village. His wife-to-be Arabella and her companions are washing pigs' innards in the stream that runs by her cottage. They taunt Jude, and Arabella attracts his attention by throwing a certain part of the pig's anatomy at him. A waterside cottage opposite the (sadly closed) Yew Tree Inn bears the name Arabella's. However, the stream is some distance below the road in a steep-sided valley, so Arabella must have had a fine throwing arm!

Maps
Landranger 1:50,000
Sheet 174
Pathfinder 1:25,000
Sheet 1154 (SU 28/38)
Map Reference of Start/
Finish SU381865

How to get there
Follow the B4507 (signposted to Ashbury) from Wantage. A mile or so outside the town, take a left-hand turning signposted to Letcombe Regis and Letcombe Bassett (if you miss this turning, the next left will also take you to Letcombe Regis). Follow the road through Letcombe Regis village until you reach the Greyhound, on the left. The Letcombes are served by the hourly Thames Transit service 38 to and from Wantage.

Letcombe Laboratory was once owned by the Agricultural Research Centre, but now belongs to the international firm Dow Elanco which undertakes research into fungicides there. There is a nature trail through the grounds. The lake has an interesting story attached to it — a prudish former owner objected to two naked statues, and reputedly had them thrown into the lake. Such a story might normally be dismissed as fanciful, but in 1982 the lake was dredged and a statue of Hercules recovered. This turned out to have been carved in the 2nd century AD and was sold for £28,000!

The suffix Regis added to a place-name indicates a royal association. Letcombe's royal was King John, who had a hunting lodge nearby. Other rulers also feature in the village's history — the manor was passed from Edward the Confessor to William the Conqueror. More recently (in 1871, to be exact) a visiting Maori chieftain named George King Hispango died here at the age of 19, and is commemorated by an obelisk in the churchyard.

The origins of Letcombe are more obscure, but most of the theories agree that the 'combe' part simply refers to the steep-sided valley between the two villages. Lyd or Lede was a generic word for a stream or leat, but some writers state that this particular stream was known as the Let. A more colourful (if implausible) explanation has it that, on seeing blood running down the hill from a great battle at Segsbury Castle, villagers shouted

Hardy country — Arabella's cottage, Letcombe Bassett

'Let the blood come! Let it come! Let come!' Letcombe Regis was formerly known as Down or Lower Letcombe. Its sister village Letcombe Bassett was known, logically enough, as Upper Letcombe. It lies a mile or so up the valley, at the head of the combe and beneath the ridge of the Downs.

The Basset family received the manor from Robert d'Oilly (builder of Oxford Castle) in around 1158. As well as its Hardy connection, the village has a link with another famous writer. Jonathan Swift, author of *Gulliver's Travels*, stayed here in 1714 as a guest of the rector, and wrote beneath a mulberry tree in the Old Rectory garden. He does not appear to have enjoyed his stay, however, and moved to Ireland after three months.

Another person who was less than keen on Letcombe Bassett was one Thomas Sharp of the planning authority, who in 1948 called the place 'a slum'. This was during a controversial episode that caught the national interest, when the authorities wished to resettle most of the village's inhabitants in Letcombe Regis, on account of the dilapidated state of some of the dwellings and the inadequate sewerage system. A stormy meeting was broadcast on the BBC Light Programme under the title *Letcombe Bassett: The Future of a Village*. Fortunately, the locals (backed by *The Times*, the *Architects' Journal* and poet John Betjeman who lived at nearby Farnborough) won the day, and the plan was quietly abandoned when a way was found to bring mains drainage to the village. Nowadays, of course, the old cottages and farmhouses have been modernized and the village is very popular.

A large barn at Rectory Farm near Letcombe Bassett church dates from about 1400 and is of cruck construction, whereby curved beams reach from the floor to the peak of the roof. Some of these massive beams, hewn from whole oak trunks, were said to have come from Bristol merchant ships, but their great size and age probably discount this particular local tradition.

Not on the route, but easily reached from the midway point, is the Ridgeway (or Rudge as it is sometimes known locally). This is part of the 85-mile long distance path from Avebury in Wiltshire to Ivinghoe Beacon in Bedfordshire. Segsbury Castle, an Iron Age hillfort, is about half a mile east of the nearest point on the Ridgeway.

Walk 3

Distance: *Allow two hours for this walk of three-and-a-half miles.*

From the entrance to the Greyhound car park, turn left and walk in front of the pub and past a thatched cottage dated 1698. When the main street swings round to the right of the church, keep straight on down a road that leads to the flint and thatched build-ing that now forms the

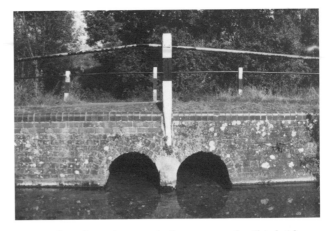

The outflow from the cress beds passes under this bridge

gatehouse to Letcombe Laboratory. Walk to the right of the thatched building, then follow a metalled path around the back of the school playground. This crosses Letcombe Brook then leads past a thatched cottage to a road. Turn left, peeping over the wall on the left for glimpses of the lake in the grounds of the Laboratory. Walk up the road for a couple of hundred yards, then turn left through Blandy's Farm. Cross Letcombe Brook again, then cross a stile into a field. Walk up the left-hand edge of the field to a further stile beneath a horse chestnut tree (notice the stone stile, now redundant). Turn right, along a path signposted as a Nature Trail. Just before a field gate, turn right into a narrow hedged path which leads back towards the stream. At the lip of the stream valley, the path swings left, then leads attractively above the valley for about half a mile, with glimpses down into the valley.

This valley (the 'combe' of Letcombe) is said to be haunted by the ghost of a disappointed lover who drowned herself in the brook. As you approach Letcombe Bassett, you pass a pretty cottage in the bottom of the valley, then you come to a stile. Take a good look at the tree that shelters the stile; most of its branches are actually those of ivy, but the hardy hawthorn supporting this massive encum-brance still just about survives. Beyond the stile the path opens out slightly; keep to the footpath, which runs tight against the fence on the left. Pass through the remains of two stiles (the second overlooking the watercress beds beyond the road on the right), then the path swings to the left and drops to the road.

A short diversion down the hill to the right leads to the watercress beds. Otherwise, cross Rectory Lane and follow the village street uphill past a hand-some brick farmhouse on the right. At a triangle (where Gramp's Hill leads off to the left), keep right. Pass a tiny chapel, which is attached to a cottage and has been converted into a stable. Arabella's cottage is just beyond it and overlooks a large pond; opposite is the former Yew Tree Inn. Keep on up the hill to Holborn

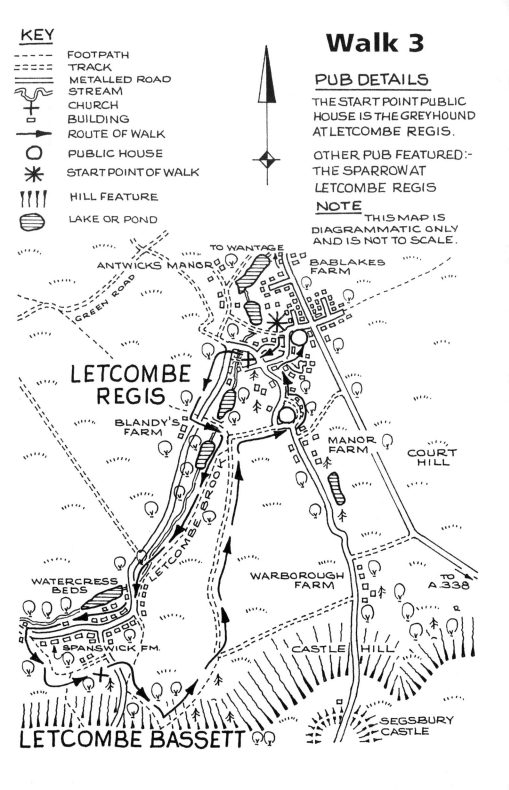

Farmhouse; here double back up the drive to Spanswick Farm on the left. Take a footpath on the right that leads between a house and the first farm building. Beyond the house there are good views to the right towards the prominent Hackpen Hill with the impressive slopes of Crowhole Bottom and the Devil's Punchbowl to its left.

The footpath leads along the edge of a field to a solitary beech tree, then swings left to a stile. Cross the stile and walk along the top edge of a field towards Letcombe Bassett church, with another handsome brick farmhouse on the left. At the end of the field is a stile into a lane, which leads between some cottages and the churchyard. Letcombe Bassett church is worth a look; the chancel arch, a blocked north doorway and two small round-headed windows in the chancel are all Norman work, and there are some old tombs in the churchyard next to the chalk-built porch.

Beyond the church, the lane meets the Gramp's Hill road; the junction is surrounded by attractive buildings (including Rectory Barn). Turn right and walk up the hill, passing a footpath sign on the left. When the road swings right, follow a signposted path on the left. Cross a stile into a field, then the path leads up slightly and then down towards the bottom of an attractive dry valley. Cross another stile and walk a few yards down the hill to a stile on the left which leads into a wood. Energetic walkers may decide to continue straight on and then climb to the Ridgeway, returning via the Smith's Hill road. Those sticking to the three-and-a-half mile route should turn left over the stile into the wood.

The wood is mainly hazel, and nuts can be gathered in autumn. The path leads through it for a couple of hundred yards, then leads over a stile out into a sheltered meadow. Keep to the right-hand edge, then cross a stile on the right into the next field, where the path continues in the same direction for about a mile. When you reach the path you trod earlier (by the stone stile under the horse chestnut tree), turn right down a hedged track. This leads shortly to the road by The Sparrow pub. Walk in front of the pub, then turn left down a village lane. Just after a white-painted thatched cottage and before you reach the end of the cul-de-sac, take a metalled path on the left. This leads between houses and gardens back to the road. Turn right and walk along the raised pavement back to Letcombe Regis church. Here turn right and walk back to the starting point. Notice the brick house on the corner, which has the date 1707 built into the wall in flint.

Villages of the Vale; Hanney, Denchworth and Grove

WALK 4
Allow 3 hours
5 ³/₄ miles
Walk begins page 25

Background to the Walk

This walk is through typical Vale of White Horse countryside — a mixture of arable fields, pasture land and the occasional flowery meadow, generally flat with wide skies and distant views to the Downs. There is a real feeling of space, particularly between West Hanney and Denchworth at the beginning of the walk. A couple of streams (Childrey Brook and Letcombe Brook) meandering across this area add interest to the landscape. As most of the walk is across farmland, paths are occasionally under crops or otherwise hard to follow. Families with young children should also note that the walk crosses the main London-Bristol railway line twice. Although visibility is good at both crossings, do please take care.

The villages are full of interest: many of the cottages are thatched, and the churches are worth investigating. In particular, West Hanney church has plenty to see. In the porch, notice the two Saxon stone coffins, and the round-headed Norman doorway (imitated by the outer Victorian arch). Inside the church is a carved Norman font and, next to it, a wall monument that solemnly records the passing of Elizabeth Bowles in 1718 at the age of 124. This is the longest recorded life-span of an Englishwoman, but has to be taken with a large pinch of salt. To the south side of the chancel arch, notice the squint and the steep stairs to the former rood loft. There are some fine old houses around the church, notably the Old Post Office (early 17th century) to the east and the stone-built Prior's Court to the west. The latter was recorded in an inventory of 1847 as being 'Stonesfield slated' (see Walk 20).

Maps
Landranger 1:50,000
Sheet 164 or 174
Pathfinder 1:25,000
Sheets 1136 (SU 49/59)
& 1135 (SU 29/39)
Map Reference of Start/
Finish SU406928

How to get there
From the A338 Wantage-
Oxford road, turn off at East
Hanney, signposted to West
Hanney, Denchworth and
Charney Bassett. Follow the
signs to West Hanney (take
care at a junction where the
left-hand turning is
signposted Through Traffic;
West Hanney is along the
right-hand road). On reaching
the village green with its
cross, take a left-hand turn to
the church. The Plough is just
past the church, on the right-
hand side. Grove and East
Hanney are served by the
hourly 31 bus from Oxford to
Wantage, operated by Thames
Transit (tel. 0865 727000).

Pub facilities
Plough, West Hanney
This is a picturesque brick and
thatch pub, a few yards from
West Hanney church. The
landlord breeds and exhibits
birds, which are on show in
aviaries in the beer garden. As
well as usual aviary species
like Canaries and Quail, he

also breeds British species, including Greenfinch, Bullfinch and Siskin. Their songs make an unusual accompaniment to your drink in the beer garden. The pub is home to a fishing club, and members of the Wilts and Berks Canal restoration society hold their meetings here. The comfortable lounge bar has an open fire (winter walkers note!), and a collection of decorative plates on the walls. In the public bar, the floor had to be lowered in one corner to give darts players sufficient headroom! This bar was once a village shop, which doubled up as the dentist's surgery. At the time of writing, the pub was between breweries, so the landlord was unsure of the range of beers that would be available, but he intends to stock as wide a range as possible. Opening hours are 1100-1500 and 1730-2300 Monday to Saturday (with slightly longer daytime hours on Saturdays), and normal Sunday hours (1200-1500, 1900-2230). Food is served seven days a week (1200-1400 and 1900-2100), described by the landlady as 'pub grub — nothing fancy'. In addition to the standard pub fare, a daily special is on offer, such as home-made steak and mushroom pie. Walkers with children are requested to use the lounge bar or garden; dog-owners are restricted to the garden. Please check with the landlord if you wish to leave your car in the car park while you walk, as space is limited at busy times.
Tel. 0235 868674.

The Plough at West Hanney

Denchworth village boasts two medieval crosses. One, merely a stump, stands in the middle of a road junction at the entrance to the village. It is thought to have been a 'chipping' or 'cheapening' cross from which chapmen (travelling pedlars) sold their wares. The thatched cottage opposite was formerly the Star public house, which closed a few years after the Second World War. The other cross, with a modern shaft and head on an old base, is in the churchyard. Like West Hanney, Denchworth church has a Norman doorway. The church was famed for its Vicar's Library, which included a Caxton edition of the Golden Legend, dated 1483 (printed just 6 years after Caxton established the first printing press in Britain, and now housed in the Bodleian Library at Oxford). Another item in the collection was catalogued as 'The Rib of a Mermaid, from Angola, 1631'. Denchworth Manor is the home of Baron Beaverbrook, Deputy Treasurer of the Conservative Party and grandson of the famous newspaper magnate. The family motto is *Res mihi non me rebus* ('Things for me, not I for things'). A row of three terraced cottages opposite The Fox was converted into a gatehouse simply by replacing the middle dwelling with a huge archway. The Beaverbrooks bought the house from Compton Mackenzie, the author of Whisky Galore, in the 1950s.

The Fox at Denchworth

A few old buildings survive in the centre of Grove village, but most of the surrounding housing is modern. Grove seems always to have been a poor relation of nearby Wantage — the Denchworth Annual of 1877 bemoans the problems the area then had in procuring a decent water supply: 'Especially bad is the case of Grove, where the people drink the sewage of Wantage'. Nowadays, Letcombe Brook is clean and children will enjoy feeding the ducks where the stream crosses the village green. These ducks are also more fortunate than their ancestors — duck races were held as part of the village feast until they were stopped by the RSPCA in the 1950s.

Walk 4

Distance: *Allow at least three hours for this walk of almost six miles.*

(Note: There are no hills, but some of the paths may be rather overgrown.) From the Plough, turn right, away from the church. Keep along Church Street, past footpaths leading off to the right and left. At Rose Cottage the road bends to the right; from this bend take the bridleway signposted to the left. Ignoring another bridleway that joins from the left, follow the track through open fields. Typical farmland birds may be seen along this stretch: Yellowhammers, Lapwings,

Fox, Denchworth

A splendid whitewashed and thatched pub opposite the church in Denchworth village, with honeysuckle growing around the door. A date-stone on the chimney reads 1688. When first obtained by Morland's over 100 years ago, the pub only occupied one end of the building (where the main bar is now); the rest contained a bakehouse, a forge and a cottage. The bakehouse and forge have since been incorporated into the pub and the latter now houses an attractive beamed restaurant. There is a large, safe garden for children, with tables and a set of swings. Morland's Old Speckled Hen and Original bitters are on sale, as is their Revival mild. Stella Artois and Foster's lagers, Guinness and Olde English cider are also available on draught. The restaurant and bar menus offer very good value. Starters include deep-fried brie in cranberry sauce, Japanese-style breaded king prawns and dim sum. Walkers may prefer snacks, such as warm filled baguettes. The bar menu offers pub staples such as lasagne and gammon, while the restaurant menu includes honey roast half duckling and grilled plaice. A typical special might be a home-made pie or a turkey curry. Vegetarians are also catered for. Food is served from 1200 to 1400 and from 1900 to 2130 (except Sunday evenings). Standard opening hours apply. Children are welcome inside the pub, but dog-owners are requested to use the garden. Most credit cards are accepted. Tel. 0235 868258.

The cheapening cross at Denchworth

Skylarks and the occasional Curlew (more likely to be heard than seen). About half a mile from the road, the path crosses a ditch at the end of a small belt of conifers. Directly ahead of you, in the distance, the Downs rise towards the hillfort at Uffington. After a further quarter-mile, at the top of a slight rise, keep straight on where another track (leading to the ruin of Hill Barn on the left) crosses at right-angles. Eventually, the bridleway emerges onto a metalled road. Turn right, and shortly you will see the Denchworth sign. Cross the road bridge over the Childrey Brook, and pass an impressive series of thatched barns on the left, until you reach the first of Denchworth's two crosses. Turn left here and walk along the village street to the Fox.

The path continues past the pub, then turns left into the churchyard (this path is signposted to Grove). At the end of the churchyard, a kissing gate leads into a pleasant grassy field, where a path straight ahead leads down to a gate by Childrey Brook. Cross the brook by the footbridge, then continue straight on towards a farm gate at the top of the field. A second gate ahead leads to the minor road from Denchworth to Grove; take the bridlepath directly opposite, again signposted to Grove. This leads diagonally across several fields, with Hill Barn again visible on the left. As you approach the railway, the path leads to the right of a rounded clump of trees surrounding a pond. Please take care crossing the railway — this is the main line from London to Bristol. Once across the railway, the path leads

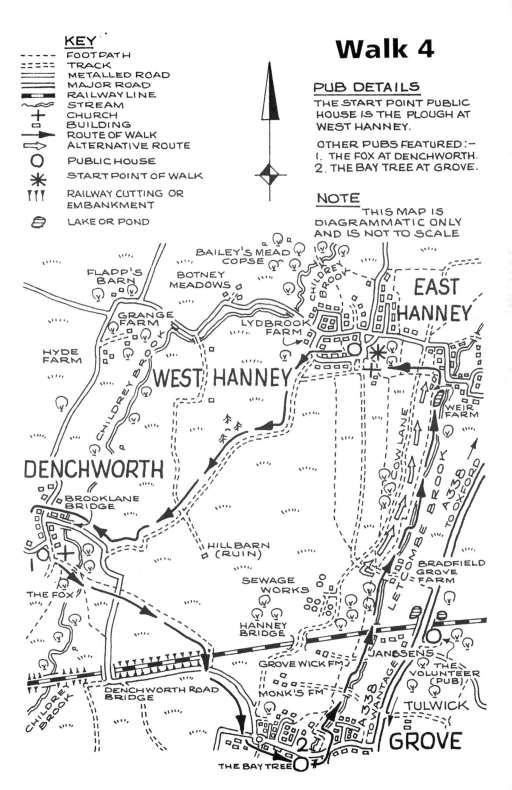

through another field to regain the lane you crossed earlier. A sign on the gate here reads 'Please Close the Gate', which seemed a little superfluous when I last walked this path, as the gate was firmly padlocked!

Turn left and walk along the road into Grove, passing the new Parish Cemetery on the left. When you reach the houses, keep straight on, passing The Maples on the left and Churchward Close on the right. At a T-junction, turn left into Newlands Drive, then keep straight on at a mini-roundabout. A hundred yards farther on, you reach the Bay Tree pub and Letcombe Brook. Cross the brook, then follow it left to a two-arched brick footbridge, where you return to the left-hand bank. An old cottage on the right has been weatherproofed with corrugated iron, but looks quaint nonetheless; a cottage on the left is more traditionally clad in brick and timber. Fifty yards on, the path leaves the stream briefly by some swings, but returns to it shortly by a metal fence. The path leads attractively through a series of flowery meadows to a metalled lane. Beyond this, the path continues in a similar vein (the brick building visible to the right is the headquarters of Janssen, the drug company), until you reach a second farm lane, where again you keep straight on with Letcombe Brook on your right. When you reach the railway, cross the tracks carefully, then walk right for a few yards to find the continuation of the path. This continues parallel to the stream as before.

After a further series of stiles, you reach a concrete track, with Bradfield Grove Farm on the right. Turn left along this track for a few yards, then, by a telegraph pole, there is an indistinct path leading across the field to the right. (The next couple of fields may be overgrown or under crops and tricky to cross. If the path looks unpromising, keep on the concrete path until you reach an obvious track, Cow Lane. Turn right and after half a mile rejoin the described route at the beginning of the next paragraph.) If you decide to brave the fields, head for the far right-hand corner, then into a further field. Walk along the right-hand edge until you reach a rather overgrown corner, where there is a footbridge followed by a stile. Walk along the edge of a field to a further gate. The path then continues pleasantly through grassy meadows, with the outlying buildings of East Hanney appearing ahead of you. A line of old willow trees on the right marks the course of a dry ditch. When you reach a field gate, aim to the right of the corrugated iron barn in front of you, with the stream close on your right. When you reach the barn, cut straight across the farmyard through two gates (the stream runs through the near corner). Beyond the farm, when you reach a line of telegraph wires, take the signposted path to your left. (East Hanney can be visited via a path between cottages to the right.)

At the end of the field, cross a stile into Cow Lane. Continue straight over via another stile. West Hanney church is straight ahead of you now — just a couple more stiles to climb! When you reach the churchyard, follow the path around the church to emerge in Church Street, with the Plough a few yards away.

Newbridge — where Thames meets Windrush

WALK 5
Allow 2 ½ hours
4 ½ miles
Walk begins page 32

Background to the Walk

This walk offers fine views, a quiet stretch of towpath, and some pleasant fieldside walking in the Upper Thames valley. The Thames as it passes below Longworth is much narrower than at Oxford. The difference in volume is mainly accounted for by the contributions of three tributaries — the Windrush (which meets the Thames at Newbridge), the Evenlode and the Cherwell. The Thames is generally considered navigable to Lechlade, but the stretches above Oxford (where the river is often known as the Isis) are considerably less busy than those below.

The walk begins in Longworth, which is a stone-built village (as are most of its neighbours in this area on the Cotswold fringe). The village was originally known simply as Worth; the Long part was added to denote its extended shape. The church, not far from the Blue Boar, dates back to the 12th century, though little of this date remains. Within the church are fragments of a monument to the Marten family, who lived at Marten's Hall Farm. Henry Marten is said to have signed King Charles I's death warrant in 1649, and tradition has it that the monument was slighted when Charles II came to the throne. Also in the church are 15th-century brasses to Richard Yate and to John Hinde. Hinde was rector of Longworth and died in 1422. Two later rectors of Longworth bore sons who found fame. The first was John Fell, born in 1625, who later became Dean of Christ Church, Oxford. Dr Fell once challenged a student to translate an epigram by the 1st-century Latin poet Martial, or be sent down. The quick-witted student paraphrased the epigram thus: 'I do not

Maps
Landranger 1:50,000
Sheet 164
Pathfinder 1:25,000
Sheets 1135 (SU 29/39),
1136 (SU 49/59),
1116 (SP 40/50)
and 1115 (SP 20/30)
Map Reference of Start/
Finish SU389995

How to get there
Longworth lies just north of the A420 between Oxford and Faringdon. Take the A415 towards Witney at a roundabout on the Kingston Bagpuize bypass section of the A420. Turn left at a crossroads, signposted to Longworth and Hinton Waldrist. Take the first right (Cow Lane) and follow the road around to the left in the village. Tuck's Lane is on the right, and the Blue Boar is a few yards down on the right-hand side. There are two infrequent bus services to Longworth village: the Oxford Bus Company's service 42 and the Swindon and District route 66.

Pub facilities
Blue Boar, Longworth
(Pictured right)
This ivy-grown pub in a quiet village lane has an attractive part-thatched exterior and a comfortable interior. The latter is enlivened by a collection of mainly agricultural implements, posters and prints around the walls, pairs of skis along the beams of the ceiling, and a less-than-traditional stuffed head over the fireplace. The pub is a Morrell's house, with their Best bitter available on draught (alongside Guinness, Harp lager and Strongbow cider). No fewer than 32 different whiskies can be sampled. Meals often include vegetables grown in the pub garden. Starters include deep-fried Camembert with cranberry sauce. In addition to the regular menu, which includes steak sandwiches and pasta dishes, specials might be seafood and sole parcels or chicken satay. Vegetarians are also catered for. Well-behaved children are welcome, as are dogs (provided they get on with Boot, the pub dog!). Most major credit cards are accepted. Tel. 0865 820494.

The two Morland's pubs at Newbridge, the Maybush and the Rose Revived, are popular and widely known. Both have riverside gardens, and either makes an excellent refreshment stop halfway round the walk.

like thee, Doctor Fell / The reason why I cannot tell / But this I know and know full well / I do not like thee, Doctor Fell' and presumably escaped punishment for his daring. The second famous rector's son was Richard Doddridge Blackmore, author of *Lorna Doone*, who was born at the rectory in 1825.

Longworth Manor (note the engine plate from the Manor Class steam locomotive that bore its name) is of the late 17th century, but was remodelled in 1910.

The Blue Boar is a Grade II listed building with an original fireplace. An account exists of a land auction being held here 'by the candle' — a pin was pushed through a lighted candle, and the land went to the highest bidder when the pin fell from the melted wax.

Newbridge, despite its name, is one of the oldest bridges on the river, although probably not *the* oldest — this distinction is usually claimed for Radcot Bridge, a few miles upstream. Newbridge's pointed arches are a good clue to its age — such arches were rarely used after the 15th century. The first written evidence of the existence of a bridge here dates from 1279, when a list of employees of Standlake Manor included a reference to 'Thomas at Pontum', probably the tollkeeper. There is a record of repairs to the bridge made in 1415 and again in 1462, when one Thomas Briggs, who lived in a hermitage at the Standlake end of the bridge, was licensed to extract tolls from passers-by to pay for the repair. A little later, during the reign of Henry VIII, Leland describes the bridge's 'six great arches of stone' in his *Itinerary*. Tolls were levied until 1600. During the Civil War, the Parliamentarians under Sir William Waller were attempting to encircle Oxford and there was a skirmish at the bridge. The Royalists ran out of ammunition and the Parliamentarians secured a passage to Abingdon, which led to Charles I retreating in disguise from his stronghold at Oxford. The bridge was damaged during the engagement but was repaired yet again and has served travellers well since. Two of the arches still retain their original ribs, yet in 1878 the county surveyor declared 'it is now a sound and trustworthy structure...the arches are as strong as when they were built'. It was given a life expectancy of at least another 300 years in 1981, when the County Council surveyed the bridge as fit to carry 32-ton lorries. The Grade I listing describes it as 'the most complete medieval bridge in Oxfordshire'. Its warm-coloured Taynton stone arches are best appreciated from the gardens of the pubs at each end, The Maybush and The Rose Revived.

The unusual name of the latter pub has several rival explanations. Perhaps the most romantic (and that favoured by the artist who painted the inn sign) is that it commemorates a visit by Cromwell, who, passing through, noticed that the rose in his buttonhole had wilted. He placed it in a tankard of ale, whereupon it returned to its former glory. More prosaically, it seems that the pub, originally called The Rose and situated directly opposite the Maybush on the southern bank, burned down and was rebuilt in its present location — hence Revived. Take time to shelter from the traffic in one of the cutwaters of the bridge to admire the view of the two pubs, the Thames and its pleasure boats, and the clear, visibly faster waters of the Windrush 'chattering for the last time over bars of golden gravel' (Joanna Cannan). Local historian and photographer Henry Taunt said contemptuously of the Windrush 'it is not navigable, and the lower part of the stream is not worth exploring'. Once there were plans to canalise the river as far as Witney, but these did not bear fruit. There is a popular but unofficial bathing place just upriver by the A415 where the Windrush and the mill leat reunite below Newbridge Mill.

The return from Newbridge to Longworth incorporates a pleasant stretch of the Thames towpath. Many of the willow trees along this stretch are pollarded. This ancient practice involves lopping off the smaller branches above head height every seven to ten years; the cut branches were used for firewood, hurdles and even for feeding livestock. The pollard (the crown of cut branches) at the top of these old willows provides nesting holes for many bird species: Tree Sparrows (the House Sparrow's rarer brown-headed cousin) and Little Owls find them particularly attractive. However, without regular maintenance, pollarded trees are liable to split or die and lose their wildlife value. Along the Thames you may see typical riparian bird species such as Kingfisher, Reed Bunting and Grey Heron. Less predictable perhaps is the occasional Common Tern (this species breeds at Farmoor Reservoir and is becoming more common along the river). The reeling song of the Grasshopper Warbler has also been heard recently in the locality. Once you leave the riverbank, the route leads just below the wooded summit of Harrowdown Hill, from where there are distant views beyond Newbridge to Boars Hill, Cumnor Hurst and Wytham Wood. Longworth, journey's end, is also visible at the top of the river terrace.

Walk 5

Distance: *Allow two-and-a-half hours for this easy countryside and riverbank walk of four-and-a-half miles.*

From the Blue Boar in Tuck's Lane, return to the main village street and turn left. Pass the entrances to Longworth School and Bow Bank Close. When the road bends right take the signposted footpath on the left between two white-painted houses, which leads to the derelict Sudbury Farm. Skirt around the left-hand edge of the farm then, when you reach a double line of Scots Pines by Draycott Moor Farm, walk between the trees to a metalled track. The large stone slab here is an old stile. Turn left along this track and enjoy the wide views over the Thames valley. When the track bends left at the end of the farm, keep straight on down a bridleway. Shortly afterwards, you pass a house entrance on the right.

Half a mile on, just short of a line of telegraph poles, you will see a three-pointed bridleway sign. The building marked on older maps (a thatched cattle shed) has been demolished. Turn right along a hedge, passing a concrete water trough, and keep alongside the hedge through a couple of fields. When you reach a field with a small wood at its far end and the main road running along its right-hand edge, head for the far right-hand corner. Here a gate and a gap in the hedge (by a bridleway signpost) lead on to the A415. Turn left towards the traffic lights at Newbridge. Take care on this short stretch, as the verges are narrow and the road is busy — keep dogs and children on a tight rein!

When you reach the Maybush, take a footpath on the left alongside the pub. This leads to a grey-painted gate and a footbridge. The path then joins the river on the right. Turn around to admire the venerable arches of Newbridge behind you, then walk along the riverbank away from the bridge. Pass Newbridge Farm a field away on your left and a World War II pill box on the opposite bank. After a series of fields separated by NRA gates, the path drops down into a narrow belt of trees along the riverside. At the end of this pleasantly shady stretch of path, cross a footbridge with a gate at each end. The river bends away to the right, but our route keeps on in the same direction as before to reach a stile on the left, about 20 yards from the river. Turn left over this stile and an overgrown bridge to emerge in the corner of a field. Turn right and keep along the field edge, climbing very gradually towards the wooded summit of Harrowdown Hill (which is about 100 feet above river level).

In the corner of the field go through a gate into a hedged green lane. This grassy track climbs alongside the wood, then drops down again, with wide views on the left. At the end of the track, turn left when you reach the entrance to a house, then after a few yards turn right along a surfaced lane (ignore a bridleway continuing to the left). The lane climbs gradually towards the village. Follow it for about half a mile, passing two footpaths (one on either side). On the outskirts of the village, walk by some attractive cottages until you reach the Blue Boar.

If you have a little extra time, take a stroll around Longworth village; the church and manor house are at the end of Church Lane.

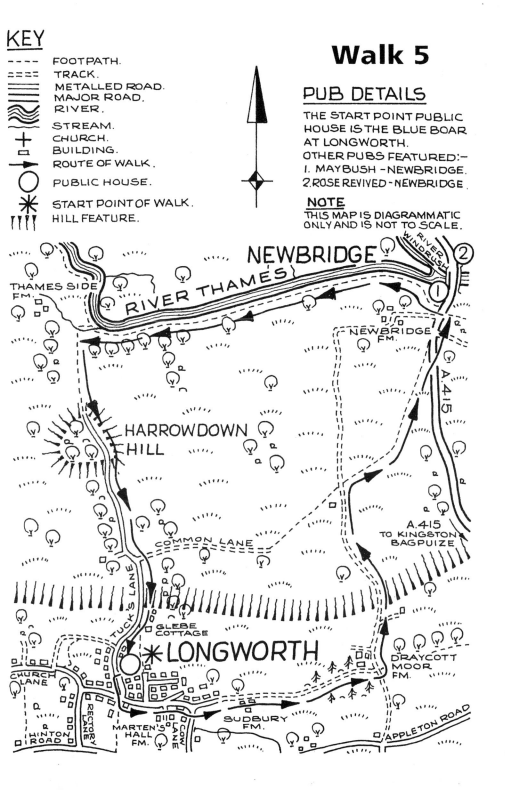

KEY

- - - -	FOOTPATH.
≡≡≡≡	TRACK.
≣≣≣	METALLED ROAD.
	MAJOR ROAD.
∿∿	RIVER.
	STREAM.
✝	CHURCH.
▫	BUILDING.
➝	ROUTE OF WALK.
○	PUBLIC HOUSE.
✳	START POINT OF WALK.
᚛᚛᚛᚛	HILL FEATURE.

Walk 5

PUB DETAILS

THE START POINT PUBLIC
HOUSE IS THE BLUE BOAR
AT LONGWORTH.
OTHER PUBS FEATURED:–
1. MAY BUSH – NEWBRIDGE.
2. ROSE REVIVED – NEWBRIDGE.

NOTE
THIS MAP IS DIAGRAMMATIC
ONLY AND IS NOT TO SCALE.

NEWBRIDGE

RIVER WINDRUSH

THAMES SIDE FM.

RIVER THAMES

NEWBRIDGE FM.

A.415

HARROWDOWN HILL

A.415
TO KINGSTON
BAGPUIZE

COMMON LANE

TUCK'S LANE

GLEBE COTTAGE

✳ LONGWORTH

DRAYCOTT MOOR FM.

CHURCH LANE

RECTORY LANE

HINTON ROAD

MARTEN'S HALL FM.

COW LANE

SUDBURY FM.

APPLETON ROAD

A wooded walk from Finstock to the Lady Well

Maps

*Landranger 1:50,000
Sheet 164
Pathfinder 1:25,000
Sheet 1091 (SP 21/31)
Map Reference of Start/
Finish SP362162*

How to get there

*Finstock lies off the B4022
between Witney and
Charlbury. The village can
also be reached from
Woodstock via Stonesfield.
Turn off the B4022 by the
Crown Inn and follow School
Road down the hill to the
Plough Inn. The village is
served by Worths Motor
Service bus routes 69, 70 and
71 (tel. 0608 677322 for
details). Finstock Station on
the Oxford-Worcester railway
line is about a mile from the
starting point.*

Pub facilities

*Plough Inn, Finstock
This thatched inn has served
travellers since 1772. It has an
attractive beamed interior
with an inglenook fireplace,
and a large sloping garden
with picnic tables, a swing
and a climbing frame
(children are welcome in the
garden, and inside the pub
with dining parents). Hook
Norton Best, Old Hooky and
Adnam's Broadside, are
regulars, supplemented by a*

Background to the Walk

Wychwood Forest once stretched from Woodstock to Burford. As in Sherwood Forest, the game was reserved for the king, and there were harsh penalties for poachers. Unlike Robin Hood and his men, however, the inhabitants of Finstock were a lawless and ungallant bunch. As late as 1809 the Secretary to the Board of Agriculture, Arthur Young, reported that 'the vicinity around Wychwood is filled with poachers, deer stealers, thieves and pilferers of every kind and Oxford Gaol would be uninhabited were it not for this fertile crime.' A favourite method of poaching was to bury garden forks at carefully chosen places in the Forest with tines sticking up to impale the leaping deer. Hollow haystacks and even the roofs of local churches were used to store the carcases before they were transported to Witney and elsewhere for sale.

As well as poachers, highwaymen and robbers frequented the area and, despite the regular traffic of drovers leading their stock between the west and London, there was said to be a certain amount of inbreeding among the local population. The Crown Inn (not on the route described here, but only a short distance from the starting point) had a particularly unsavoury reputation: one 18th-century landlord was something of a rogue himself, and allowed highwaymen to divvy up their loot at the pub. Until 1967 there was a door at the top of the stairs that had a gap at the top to allow the occupants to shoot at any uninvited villains who broke into the building.

Lord Churchill stopped the annual Wychwood Fair in the 1850s (after earlier fairs had attracted pickpock-

The Plough at Finstock

guest beer. The selection of wines available by the glass is a cut above the ordinary; there is also a good range of malt whiskies. The food menu often includes seasonal vegetables and fresh fish. As well as bar snacks and the regular menu, a large variety of specials are offered. When we called in, the specials were Kleftico (Greek leg of lamb slow-cooked with fresh herbs and spices), king prawns and shallots, home-made vegetarian pie and fresh tortellini with Parma ham and Parmesan cheese. On Sundays, you can also choose from one or more roast dinners. Patrons are permitted to leave their cars at the pub, but it would be courteous to let the bar staff know before departing; non-pubgoing walkers should park thoughtfully elsewhere. Opening hours are 1200-1430 and 1800-2330 Monday to Friday. The pub is open all day on Saturdays and Bank Holidays; on Sundays, normal restricted hours apply. Food is served seven days a week from 1200 till 1400 and from 1900 till 2130. Accommodation is available. Tel. 0993 868333.

ets and thieves) despite its popularity — over 20,000 people, some from as far afield as Birmingham, had once attended the festivities.

The name Finstock may mean 'the place frequented by woodpeckers'; it has also been explained as meaning 'the stronghold of Fin', or the 'Fin (or fair) town'. Whatever its origins, and despite its past reputation, Finstock is now a pretty stone village with some interesting houses. John Wesley preached in the village in 1775; he was a friend of the Bolton family who lived at Manor Farm. Early Methodist meetings were held here until the Wesleyan Chapel was built in 1840. The Anglican church was built a year later on a site by the main road given by the first Baron Churchill. Jane Baroness Churchill, Lady in Waiting to Queen Victoria for 46 years, is buried in the churchyard, as is the novelist Barbara Pym, who died in 1980. Her novel *Quartet in Autumn* was shortlisted for the Booker Prize in 1977. Another famous name connected with the church was that of T. S. Eliot, who was baptised into the Church of England here in 1927. In 1894 the single church bell fell from the belfry and narrowly missed the vicar, who promptly held a service of thanksgiving.

The village hall was originally a glove factory — glove-making was an important industry in Charlbury and the surrounding villages, and still survives today on a small scale. The nearby royal hunting grounds at Wychwood and Woodstock created a demand for hunting and hawking gloves that the villages around Charlbury were well placed to meet, given the abundant local supplies of deer and sheepskin. Even the local water was considered ideal for the curing of leather. A pair of Finstock gloves were sent to the Great Exhibition of 1851.

Although the main remnant of Wychwood Forest lies to the west of the village, there are also a few relics to the east, through which this walk passes. Topples Wood takes its name from the lost village of Tapwell or Tappewell which was already in decline by 1327 (although two dwellings survived until at least the reign of Queen Elizabeth I). The remains of some village buildings and some small pits (probably stone quarries) have been excavated to the right of Topples Lane at the entrance to the wood. Woodland birds such as Great Spotted Woodpecker, Nuthatch and Goldcrest can be seen in Topples Wood and Holly Grove; a headless horseman is also said to haunt the Forest!

There are several wells and springs in the district. Finstock received its first piped water supply from the Iron Well at Fawler; before that, water had been drawn from a well in School Road (still visible, but capped). The Lady Well, surrounded by a circular wall, lies at the end of an old avenue of pollarded ash trees below the hamlet of Wilcote. It is associated with the adjacent spring, the waters of which are rich in calcium carbonate. Over the millenia, this has been deposited as a layer of tufa nearly 8 feet thick along the valley bottom below Brideswell Farm.

Between Shakenoak Farm and North Leigh Lane is the site of a Roman Villa. This is thought to have been occupied from the 1st to the 4th century AD, and was used thereafter as a Saxon burial ground and more recently as a source of stone. The site has been extraordinarily productive to archaeologists: bronze and silver coins, brooches, pottery, oyster shells, belts and buckles have been unearthed, as well as the skeletons of nine former inhabitants. Fawler village (seen near the start of the walk) gets its name from the Anglo Saxon 'fagan floran', meaning 'patterned floor'; this is taken as evidence of a mosaic on the site of another Roman villa which lay between the village and the railway.

Walk 6

Distance: *Allow between two and three hours for this countryside and woodland walk of five-and-a-half miles.*

From the inn sign of The Plough, follow the stony Dark Lane opposite. This leads down a dry valley towards the River Evenlode. The grassland on either side of the path as you approach Topples Wood is a good place to look for orchids and other flowering plants, as well as their attendant butterflies. When you reach a stile at the top of a field, turn right along a tree-lined path. Look out to the left for views of Fawler village on the opposite side of the Evenlode valley.

After a short distance, the path reaches the corner of Topples Wood. The site of Tapwell village is to the right of the path at the entrance of the wood, but there is little or nothing to be seen from the path, and the few indistinct humps and bumps that remain are concealed and inaccessible among the trees and undergrowth. The path continues pleasantly along the edge of the wood until it reaches a stand of conifers. Here it swings to the right and follows a forestry track slightly uphill through the trees. When you reach the edge of the wood, look to your left for an

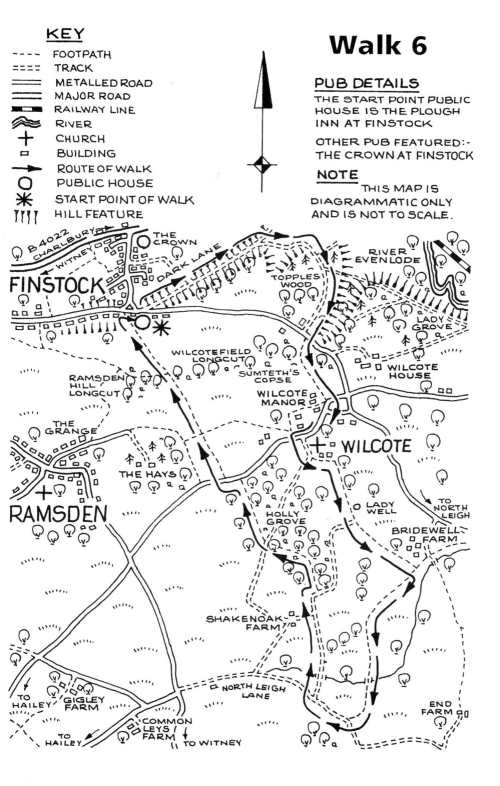

Walk 6

KEY

- `---` FOOTPATH
- `====` TRACK
- `===` METALLED ROAD
- `===` MAJOR ROAD
- RAILWAY LINE
- RIVER
- CHURCH
- BUILDING
- ROUTE OF WALK
- PUBLIC HOUSE
- START POINT OF WALK
- HILL FEATURE

PUB DETAILS

THE START POINT PUBLIC HOUSE IS THE PLOUGH INN AT FINSTOCK

OTHER PUB FEATURED:-
THE CROWN AT FINSTOCK

NOTE

THIS MAP IS DIAGRAMMATIC ONLY AND IS NOT TO SCALE.

B 4022 CHARLBURY

WITNEY

THE CROWN

DARK LANE

FINSTOCK

TOPPLES WOOD

RIVER EVENLODE

LADY GROVE

WILCOTEFIELD LONGCUT

SUMTETH'S COPSE

WILCOTE HOUSE

RAMSDEN HILL LONGCUT

WILCOTE MANOR

THE GRANGE

WILCOTE

THE HAYS

RAMSDEN

HOLLY GROVE

LADY WELL

TO NORTH LEIGH

BRIDEWELL FARM

SHAKENOAK FARM

TO HAILEY

GIGLEY FARM

NORTH LEIGH LANE

END FARM

TO HAILEY

COMMON LEYS FARM

TO WITNEY

attractive view of Wilcote House. The core of the building is 17th century, with later additions; the garden is occasionally open to the public under the National Gardens Scheme, as is that of Wilcote Manor.

As you reach the road, you pass some farm buildings on the right. One of these is used as a workshop by a lettercutter and sculptor, and samples of engraved slate are sometimes on display. When you reach the road, turn left. At the bottom of the dip, follow the path on the right signposted to Wilcote, which leads over a stile and then diagonally up the field. Follow the far edge of the field until you return to the road at a stile in front of Wilcote Manor. Turn right and walk along the road to Wilcote church. This small church was built in Norman times, but was heavily restored by the Victorians.

Fifty yards beyond the church, turn left into a farm driveway. When you reach the farm pond, take a right-hand path, then keep left around the pond, ignoring an inviting path (unfortunately not a right of way) that leads straight on towards Holly Grove (our route returns later by another path through this wood, so you will get to explore it eventually). There are often bantams and chickens scratching around at the back of the farm; the concrete track leads round the back of the farm buildings, then swings right by some old stone pigsties.

When you have left the farm buildings behind, the path starts to descend. A wide view opens up on the left, which extends as far as Brill Hill in Buckingham-shire (nearly twenty miles away) and the John Radcliffe Hospital in Headington, Oxford. The stone-built tower in the centre of the valley belongs to North Leigh church. The path leads downhill along an avenue of old ash trees until it reaches the Lady Well, almost at the bottom of the valley. Beyond the well the path crosses a gate by a spring on the left (rather muddy, but the flow is just about discernible). A stile leads into a cultivated field; walk left across the corner of the field to a gap in the hedge. From this point, aim just to the right of Brideswell Farm. At the back of the farm buildings are a series of pens containing dozens of partridges. Their released cousins can also be seen around the feeders and in the maize and millet provided for their benefit along the top edge of the field.

When you reach a stream (dammed to form a pond), turn right and aim diagonally uphill to the top right-hand corner of the field. In the corner, the path winds through a belt of trees and bushes, then passes through a 'kissing gate without the gate' into another field. The path leads along the right-hand edge of the field under a tall hedge. At the end of the field cross a stream, and skirt around the right of the next field. The field edge leads round to the right to North Leigh Lane. This attractive green lane runs from North Leigh village towards Hailey; turn right and follow it for about quarter of a mile. Keep an eye out on the right for a double field gate and a footpath sign to Wilcote. Follow this path across fields with Shakenoak Farm on the left. As you draw level with the farm, the path switches to the right-hand side of a hedge and continues towards Holly Grove. When you reach the wood, the path curves to the right for a short distance, then turns left into the wood at a gate.

The Lady Well, near Wilcote

There now follows a leafy half-mile stretch through the broad-leaved woodland of Holly Grove. Keep your eyes and ears open for the abundant birdlife among the trees, and look out for hazelnuts in the autumn. At first the path leads through the middle of the wood, but after crossing a ditch by a bridge made of railway sleepers, it runs close to the left-hand edge with the bulk of the wood rising to the right. The path is muddy in places (particularly at first) but these wet patches are usually bypassable without too much difficulty. Midway along you cross a perpendicular track in a small clearing. At the end of the wood you reach the Wilcote road.

Turn left along the road for a few steps then turn right along a footpath signposted to Finstock, just before a small disused and overgrown quarry alongside the road. The path follows a line of telegraph wires across a couple of fields. The line of Akeman Street passes from east to west here, but no modern thoroughfare follows it at this point. Roman remains have been found, indicating the position of a settlement. Pass through a strip of woodland (marked on the OS map as 'Ramsden Hill Longcut') then walk straight across the next field to the corner of a hedge. Walk down the hill with the hedge on your right and the telegraph wires to your left. In the corner a stile leads into a field with a small wood on the left and allotment gardens on the right. At the bottom of the field is a short stretch of tree-lined track then, unexpectedly, you find yourself along the edge of the back garden of The Plough.

WALK 7
Allow 2 hours
4 miles
Walk begins page 44

Along the Causeway from Steventon to Milton

Maps
Landranger 1:50,000
Sheet 164 or 174
Pathfinder 1:25,000
Sheet 1136 (SU 49/59)
Map Reference of Start/
Finish SU467917

How to get there
Steventon is easily reached by car from the A34: leave at the Milton interchange, then take the A4183 exit signposted to Wantage. Take the first right-hand turning (the B4017 to Steventon and Drayton). This road leads down Steventon Hill and crosses the railway. In the centre of the village by the green and just before the war memorial, turn left into The Causeway. The North Star is at the junction of The Causeway and Stocks Lane, opposite Steventon Primary School. Steventon can also be reached from Abingdon via Drayton, and from East Hanney via an unclassified road. The villages of Steventon and Milton are served by the hourly Thames Transit 32 and 32A services between Wantage, Didcot and Oxford.

Background to the Walk

This short walk takes a lingering look around the villages of Steventon and Milton. The centrepiece of Steventon village is a paved causeway running from one end of the village to the other, which was built for the monks of Steventon Priory. The causeway is difficult to date, but it is certainly ancient; even in 1419 responsibility for its upkeep was said to rest with the tenants of the manor 'by ancient custom'. The causeway may have been part of an ancient route to East Hendred and thence to Hungerford. It once formed the main axis of the village (hence the concentration of old cottages along it), but this shifted to the north-south road some time in the 17th century. This shift may have been due to the local market's moving from East Hendred to East Ilsley.

Of all the buildings along the causeway, probably the most interesting are the Priory Cottages near the church. These former monastic buildings, one of which includes the Great Hall of the priory, date back in parts to the 14th century. The buildings are administered by the National Trust — visits may be arranged on Wednesday afternoons (April-September) by written appointment with the occupants.

Steventon has strong links with the Great Western Railway, which passes though the village — it is halfway between London and Bristol. The stone cottages by the railway bridge were designed by Isambard Kingdom Brunel and built around 1840; they were used for board meetings. Steventon station (now closed) was for four years the nearest to Oxford, so was used by young gentlemen coming up to the University, who

The North Star at Steventon

Pub facilities
North Star, Steventon
This Morland's pub is named after the first locomotive to pass through the village on the Great Western Railway in 1837. The main line is only a hundred yards or so away. The garden is guarded by an old railway signal, and the tables and benches are painted in the green and red of the GWR. The building is believed to date back to the 1500s, and there is an unusual entrance to the garden between two fused yew trees. This pub, which has citations from CAMRA members on its walls, is an authentic country local with a humble interior and a pleasant garden served by a hatch from the bar. Food is limited to filled rolls (weekday lunchtimes only) and there is no juke-box, pool table, fruit machine or piped music. Morland's Original bitter, Revival mild and Foster's lager are available on draught, and a range of bottled beers (including Old Speckled Hen) are kept.

Walkers in search of hot food or a wider range of drinks are recommended to try any of the three pubs in the High Street near the railway bridge (**Fox**, **Cherry Tree**, **Timsbury Hotel** or **Admiral Benbow**) in Milton village.

completed their journeys by stagecoach. There were eight coaches to Oxford each day, and in 1842 well over 70,000 passengers paid the 3-shilling fee. Originally, there were plans for the railway line to Oxford to leave the main GWR line here; in the end, this dubious honour went to nearby Didcot. The route described here crosses the main line at Causeway Crossing.

Steventon once had three fulling mills; of these only Mill House (near the waterfall in Mill Street) survives. Nearby is an old barn raised on brick arches to keep the grain dry in times of flood.

Milton village was once described (in 1906) as 'the most tranquil of villages, an oasis of elm-trees at the edge of the plain of the Vale'. Nowadays, such a description would be rather kind to the village; it is now overshadowed by the nearby Milton Park Industrial Estate (built on the site of an RAF depot that was established in 1916), Didcot Power Station and the A34 trunk road. However, it still retains some attractive cottages and farmhouses. The jewel of the village is Milton Manor, built in the latter half of the 17th century. The design of the house has sometimes been attributed to Inigo Jones; this claim was made in the sale particulars when the house changed hands in 1763, so it is of long standing, but it is probably safer to describe the house as being 'in the style of' the great architect. The building was built for one Paul Calton (the Calton family had held the manor since 1546) and was complete by 1663. Milton has had a number of famous visitors. Perhaps the most important was William of Orange, who stayed here in December 1688 while his army was quartered in Abingdon. That night he heard that James II had fled the country and he left for London the next morning to pursue his claim to the throne; he was crowned the following year.

Calton later passed the house to his only son, also called Paul. By 1696 the son had allowed the building to deteriorate so badly that it was taken over by the bailiffs; he also failed to maintain his parents and sister. To add insult to injury, Paul Calton senior was summoned to the assizes at Abingdon accused of debts incurred by his son. Things got so heated at one stage that father and son almost came to blows, arming themselves with a copper pot and a chair respectively. Calton senior accused his son of cowardice, saying that he would not fight with a sword, whereupon the son grabbed a rusty sword and vowed that he would 'prick his father's pudding'. The two were eventually prevented from duelling by the intervention of a bailiff.

GWRailwayana at the North Star

The great 17th-century sailor Admiral Benbow is closely associated with Milton village, and is commemorated by the pub name (formerly the Red Lion, and before that The Dogge). Benbow started his working life as a butcher's apprentice, but ran off to sea. As a commander he is said to have decapitated 13 Moors and presented the salted heads at Cadiz in order to claim a bounty known as 'head money'. He eventually rose to the rank of Vice-Admiral, and in another incident he continued to command his fleet, despite the desertion of some of his captains, when his legs had been shattered by 'chain shot' (a device intended to destroy ships' rigging). He has been described as 'the Nelson of his time'. His house was in Deptford in London, but he owned a property known as the Dower House in Milton. The location of this house is not known for certain — it was possibly the thatched cottage next to the pub, but more likely was another property, long disappeared. While at Milton, he received a visit from Peter the Great, Czar of Russia; Benbow gave an alms-dish (marked with his punning coat of arms, a bent bow) to the church in commemoration of the visit. Benbow died in Kingston, Jamaica in 1702 and is commemorated by a monument in St. Mary's Church in Shrewsbury. His telescope and seal are preserved in Milton House. Benbow's daughter married the son of the profligate lord of the manor, yet another Paul Calton.

The causeway at Steventon

The house was bought from the Caltons by John Bryant Barrett, a London lacemaker, in 1764. Bryant Barrett, the great-great-great-grandfather of the present occupant, extended the house, dug the lake and built the gate and gateposts by the church. One of the additions made at this time was a chapel, which from the outside looks much the same as any other part of the house. This was intentional; the Barretts were devout Catholics at a time when to follow Rome was to invite persecution, so the chapel had to be quickly disguised as a normal room if necessary. It includes some stained glass said to be from Steventon church. Bryant Barrett was a friend of Bishop Richard Challenor, who is credited with ushering in a new era in English Catholic literature. When the bishop died in 1781, Bryant Barrett had his body placed in the Barrett family vault in the church, where it lay until 1946 when it was transferred to Westminster Cathedral. More recently, the Manor featured in a TV advertisement in which the subject, a car, raced behind the house to appear at both ends of a school photograph. The Manor is open to the public on two or three afternoons a week in the summer, but the precise arrangements vary from year to year — enquire locally for up-to-date information.

Milton church is one of only four in the country to be dedicated to St. Blaise, the patron saint of wool-combers (so-called because he was martyred by being torn apart with an iron wool-comb). This dedication probably reflects Milton's position on the former route from Abingdon to the sheep fair at East Ilsley. The church has a 14th-century tower, but most of the rest of the building was rebuilt in 1851 following a fire. Of interest within are a brass candelabra donated by the senior steward of New College in the 17th century, and a rare wooden coat of arms of Charles II. The church windows contain medallions of 16th-century Flemish glass. In the churchyard is the bowl and octagonal base of the old church font, which was rescued from the garden of the adjacent rectory.

At the end of the lane linking the church with the High Street is a tree planted to celebrate the Silver Jubilee of Queen Elizabeth II. A large sarsen stone known as the Stocks Stone lies nearby and marks the former location of the village stocks. The High Street was once called Potash Lane; this alkali was worked near the present-day railway bridge, and was probably carted along the High Street to Milton Mill.

Walk 7

Distance: *Allow about two hours for this village and countryside walk of about four miles.*

From the yew tree arch at the entrance to the North Star pub, cross the road and join the causeway. Walk east (towards the High Street), passing Steventon Post Office on the right and allotments on the left. Keep along the causeway until you reach the war memorial. Cross the High Street and continue along the causeway with the cricket pitch on your left. Look into a yard on the right for a glimpse of some old level crossing gates.

By a fine half-timbered house and an impressive converted barn set back from the road on the right, and just before the small compound of Steventon Pumping Station, leave the causeway and follow the metalled lane to the right. Immediately beyond the pumping station, take the bridleway on the left towards Milton. Like the

The yew tree entrance to the North Star

causeway, this path is cobbled so is dry underfoot even in the wettest weather. After a while, the path meets the Ginge Brook, quite deep and slow-moving at this point, which it follows for several hundred yards to the footbridge over the A34 dual carriageway. Once over the road, the noise of the traffic gradually diminishes as the path continues alongside the stream for a further quarter of a mile. It finally leaves the stream by the entrance to Milton Mill, where you bear right. The track then runs alongside the wall of Milton Manor, with a field of broad ridge and furrow on the left. At the end of a lean-to greenhouse on the other side of the wall, turn right through a staggered metal barrier into a path with high brick walls on either side. This leads shortly to Milton church. Pass the end of the churchyard to emerge in a lane near the Admiral Benbow pub. Opposite, pass through a kissing gate into a small paddock with the wall of the Manor on the right, and the backs of the houses of Milton village on the left. At the end of the field, a further kissing gate leads to a short stretch of walled path. Beyond this the route swings left behind a row of terraced cottages into an alley known as Little Lane, which emerges shortly in the High Street. Turn right past the last of the recently installed traffic-calming chicanes and walk down the High Street. Beyond an old orchard on the right, and opposite an imposing farmhouse (Millbrook House), turn right

KEY

- - - - FOOTPATH.
==== TRACK.
═══ METALLED ROAD.
≡≡≡ MAJOR ROAD.
▬▬ RAILWAY.
∿∿ STREAM.
✝ CHURCH.
▫ BUILDING.
➤ ROUTE OF WALK.
◯ PUBLIC HOUSE.
✳ START POINT OF WALK.
⊜ LAKE OR POND.
╽╽╽╽ HILL FEATURE.

Walk 7

PUB DETAILS

THE START POINT PUBLIC
HOUSE IS THE NORTH STAR
AT STEVENTON.
OTHER PUBS FEATURED:-
1. ADMIRAL BENBOW – MILTON
2. CHERRY TREE – STEVENTON.
3. FOX – STEVENTON.
4. TIMSBURY HOTEL-STEVENTON.

NOTE

THIS MAP IS DIAGRAMMATIC
ONLY AND IS NOT TO SCALE.

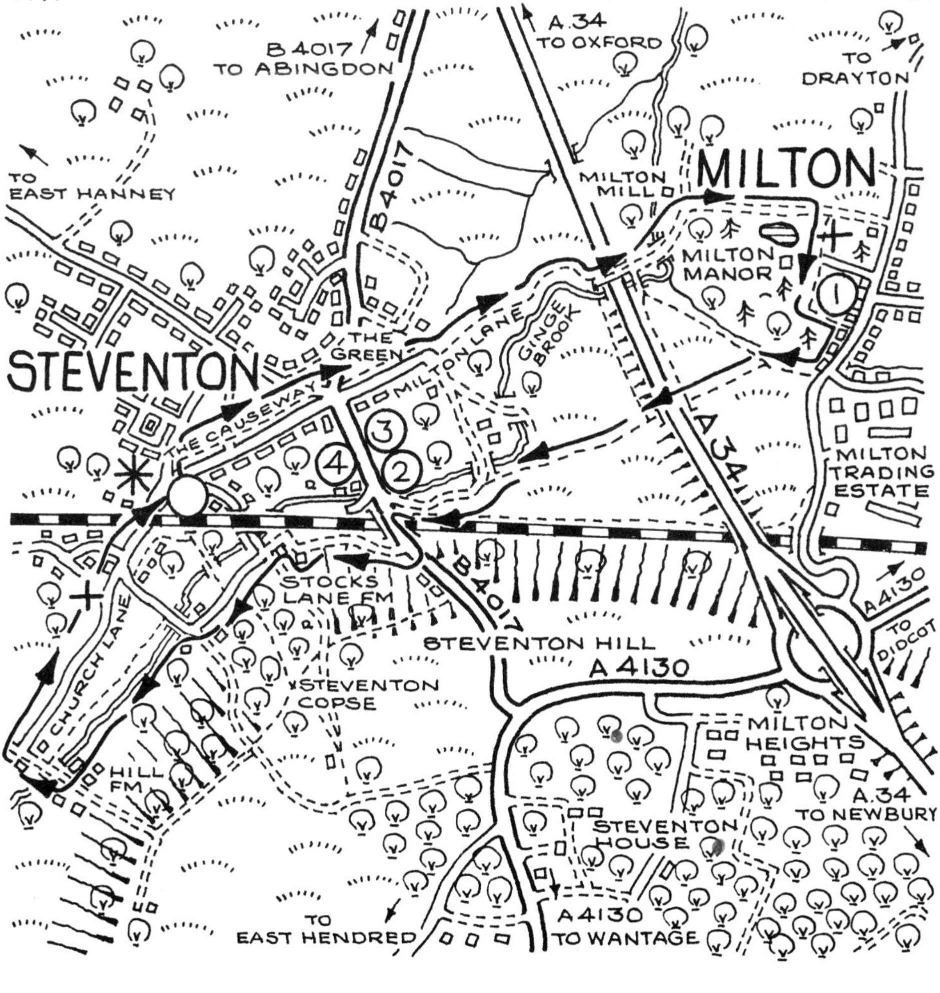

B 4017
TO ABINGDON

A.34
TO OXFORD

TO
DRAYTON

TO
EAST HANNEY

MILTON
MILL

MILTON

MILTON
MANOR

B 4017

MILTON
LANE

GINGE
BROOK

THE
GREEN

STEVENTON

THE CAUSEWAY

MILTON LANE

A.34

MILTON
TRADING
ESTATE

CHURCH LANE

STOCKS
LANE FM

B 4017

A 4130

STEVENTON HILL
A 4130

STEVENTON
COPSE

MILTON
HEIGHTS

A.34
TO NEWBURY

HILL
FM

STEVENTON
HOUSE

TO
EAST HENDRED

A 4130
TO WANTAGE

over a footbridge into a shady area of trees surrounded by streams. Two park benches here make a pleasant spot for a rest. A stile shows the way on, along a field edge with trees to the right. At the end of this field, a further stile leads into a pasture; head more-or-less straight ahead to a stile by the tunnel under the A34. Once through the tunnel, aim for the far left-hand corner of the field ahead of you. A slightly overgrown section leads through the hedge to a field which has the railway running along its southern side. Turn right and walk along the northern edge of the field for quarter of a mile or so.

Just before you reach a line of telegraph wires, turn towards the stream on your right. Don't miss the charming stone bridge over the stream, but do not cross it; instead turn left and walk along a grassy path. When this emerges into a metalled lane (Pugsden Lane), keep straight on past a number of houses and smallholdings. Just short of the High Street the lane bends to the right to emerge by the Cherry Tree pub. The Fox and the Timsbury Hotel are nearby.

To continue the walk, cross the High Street and turn left over the railway bridge, passing the entrance to the former GWR cottages by the new Jehovah's Witnesses' Kingdom Hall on the right. Immediately over the bridge, take a stony track on the right which leads down to the railway. The track runs parallel to the railway line for a short while then leads away from it slightly to skirt around Stocks Lane Farm. The farmhouse was built in the 16th century, but its age is obscured by a timbered façade of around 1900. When you reach Stocks Lane, walk straight on along Castle Street until it bends to the right into Mill Street. The area of woodland overlooking the village on the left is known as Steventon or Ladypiece Copse and contains a huge crab apple tree, one of the largest specimens in the country.

Walk along Mill Street for a few yards, then take a path on the left next to a small waterfall. This path leads between gardens with the old mill beyond the stream on the left, to a footbridge over a side-stream (often dry). Cross the footbridge and keep along the stream, passing some large poplar trees between the path and the stream. When you reach Hill Farm, leave the stream and turn right to reach Church Lane. Turn back parallel, but in the opposite direction, to the way you came. Walk along the lane for about a quarter of a mile to Steventon church (which may come as a surprise to some users of the Oxford OS map, as it is omitted from some editions!). Walk past the church and rejoin the causeway by the Priory Cottages (on the right). The remaining section of the causeway is lined with fine timbered and plastered houses. Midway back to the North Star, you cross the railway at the level crossing, from which it is a short distance back to your starting point.

To Abingdon Abbey from Sutton Courtenay

WALK 8
Up to 5 hours
8 miles
Walk begins page 49

Background to the Walk

This walk goes through Abingdon, the administrative centre of the Vale of White Horse, and two of its satellite villages. The route follows three waterways (the Thames, the Ock and Ginge Brook) for a significant proportion of the walk, and crosses the line of another, the defunct Wilts and Berks Canal. The Canal was opened in 1810, and linked the Thames at Abingdon with the Kennet and Avon Canal near Trowbridge forming an important link between the Midlands and the West Country. The canal fell into disuse in the early part of this century. Little now remains to be seen in this area, but the line of the canal is visible near New Cut Mill and a cast-iron bridge over the Ock next to the Old Anchor Inn in Abingdon is inscribed ERECTED BY THE WILTS & BERKS CANAL COMPANY AD 1824.

The closure of the canal contributed to the decline of the Thames as a cargo route. However, the river at Abingdon is still busy with pleasure boats, rowing eights and even the occasional yacht. The view of the river and town from Abingdon Bridge is memorable. It includes the Napoleonic Old Gaol (now a Sports and Leisure Centre) and the spire of St. Helen's Church. In the shadow of the church are the Old Malthouse (with a window projecting over the river) and The Old Anchor Inn on St. Helen's Wharf.

St. Helen's Church is unusual in that it is wider than it is long. It contains a unique 13th-century painted ceiling representing the Tree of Jesse. Also unique is the set of almshouses in the churchyard. There are three blocks of almshouses: Twitty's (1707), Long Alley (1446)

Maps
Landranger 1:50,000
Sheet 164
Pathfinder 1:25,000
Sheet 1136 (SU 49/59)
Map Reference of Start/
Finish SU505942

How to get there
Take the A415 from Abingdon towards Dorchester. Turn right by the Waggon and Horses pub, signposted to Sutton Courtenay and Didcot. Cross the River Thames at Culham Lock, then turn right when you reach the outskirts of Sutton Courtenay village. Drive round a sharp left-hand bend. The George and Dragon pub is about 100 yards down on the left, by the church; please park in the public car park signposted on the left just beyond the pub. Thames Transit services 32 and 32A serve Sutton Courtenay, Drayton and Abingdon; walkers who start the walk from Abingdon will have a wider choice of buses. For train travellers, Appleford Halt (on the Didcot-Oxford line) is a mile or so from the beginning of the route.

Pub facilities
George and Dragon,
Sutton Courtenay
(Pictured right)
On the edge of the village
green next to the church, the
George and Dragon has a fine
location in the heart of Sutton
Courtenay village. The
building dates back to 1570,
and has been a public house
for most of that time. The
central bar by which
customers now enter was
formerly the snug and the rest
of the pub was to the right,
where the restaurant is now.
The main bar to the left was
added when the pub absorbed
an adjoining cottage. It is said
that Herbert Asquith, the
Liberal prime minister, used
to frequent the George and
Dragon, and on occasion hid
in the cellar when Lady
Asquith came looking for him.
The George is a Morland's
pub, and serves their Old
Speckled Hen and Original
bitters, as well as Revival
mild. The landlord also has
plans to introduce guest beers.
The draught lagers on sale are
Stella Artois and Foster's;
Guinness and Olde English
cider complete the draught
line-up. In addition, up to 30
malt whiskies are available,
and five or six wines are
served by the glass (and many
more by the bottle). A wide
variety of good food is served,
home-made pies being
something of a speciality.
Soup, sandwiches, jacket
potatoes and ploughman's
lunches will suit those in
search of a lighter meal, and
vegetarians may be tempted by
dishes such as cheese and leek
pie or Neapolitan pasta bake.
Opening hours are 1100-1500
and 1800-2300 (except
Sundays, 1200-1500 and

with its wooden cloister and cupola, and Brick Alley (1718). Also of architectural interest in Abingdon is the County Hall in the Market Place. This was designed by Christopher Kempster (a pupil of Christopher Wren) and built in 1678-82. The first floor houses the town's museum, which includes among its exhibits the fossilised bones of an ichthyosaur recently discovered in a nearby gravel pit, and a set of wrist and ankle irons from the Old Gaol. The paved area on the ground floor between the pillars was, and still is, used as a market.

The Benedictine Abbey at Abingdon was founded in the 7th century and once controlled much of the surrounding area. The most interesting of the few remaining buildings are seen from this route. Firstly, the Abbey Gateway and the adjoining church of St. Nicholas (built in the 15th and 12th centuries respectively) overlook the Market Place. The Checker or Exchequer (with its fine gabled chimney) and the Long Gallery (built around 1500) are nearby — the walk passes though a passageway between the Checker and the Unicorn Theatre. The latter, which occupies what seems to have been an open hall associated with the Checker building, has a 15th-century roof and a replica Elizabethan stage.

A tributary crossed by the Thames towpath at Culham tollhouse is marked on the OS map as the Back Water, but locals know it as Swift Ditch. It is crossed by three bridges close to its confluence with the Thames —

the footbridge carrying the towpath; a modern bridge carrying the A415 Abingdon-Dorchester road; and, between the two, the original Culhamford bridge of 1416. The bridge was built of stone from Sandford and the labourers who worked on it are said to have received a penny a day, a high wage in those days. The view of the bridge and adjacent tollhouse from the footbridge is one of the highlights of the walk. Swift Ditch was used by river traffic in the 17th and 18th centuries, and there is evidence that it was improved for navigation by the monks of Abingdon Abbey.

1900-2230). Well-behaved children are welcome, but dog-owners are requested not to bring their animals inside the building. Tel. 0235 848252. There is limited car parking available in front of the pub — you are best advised to park in the public car park on the village green nearby.

*There are two riverside pubs in Abingdon, the **Old Anchor Inn** on St Helen's Wharf and the **Nag's Head** on the bridge. This walk passes both of them. There are also several pubs in the town centre.*

The churches of Drayton and Sutton Courtenay are interesting. St. Peter's, Drayton, has an aumbry (or wall cupboard) which retains its original door, one of only three in the country to do so. Of these three, Drayton's is unique in that the lock survives and is still functional. There is also an alabaster reredos or altar back of around 1400, which probably only survives because it was hidden to prevent it being desecrated by the Puritans — it was discovered under the church floor in 1814. Sutton Courtenay church has a Norman tower, font and chancel arch, and an attractive Perpendicular brick porch. In the churchyard are the tombs of Eric Blair (better known as George Orwell, the author of *1984* and *Animal Farm*) and Herbert Asquith, Liberal prime minister from 1908 to 1916. Also in Sutton Courtenay, opposite the church and the George and Dragon pub, is Norman Hall, a stone-built manor house of around 1200 and a rare survival.

The birdlife you are likely to see is predominantly aquatic. Both the Thames and the Ock attract typical riverside birds such as Kingfishers and Grey Herons. The Thames between Abingdon and Culham hosts a large flock of Mute Swans for much of the year, but less obvious species such as Sedge Warbler (summer only) and Reed Bunting may also be seen along this stretch. Great Crested Grebes breed at Sutton Pools, a series of weir pools which (particularly when the river is high) forms an exciting climax to the walk.

Walk 8

Distance: *Allow between four and five hours for this eight-mile walk through town, village and countryside with much architectural interest.*

Turn left from the George and Dragon, past the gate to the church, then keep along the main road (Church Street) until you reach the Triangle. Take the right-hand turning (Brook Street) which quite shortly crosses Ginge Brook. Beyond the bridge, turn left at a footpath sign into a driveway alongside the stream. This leads to a mill (from a path to the left, the stream can be seen emerging from an archway under the mill house). Keep to the *right* of the mill house through a kissing gate into a field. Walk parallel to the stream to a stile in the hedge on the far side of the field.

Beyond this hedge, walk alongside the stream which meanders attractively through the field to a stile and footbridge in the near corner. This leads to a track (East Way). Turn right, passing a couple of smallholdings on the left.

Follow East Way for about half a mile to a road, ignoring a footpath that crosses it at right-angles near Hulgrove Farm. Cross the road and continue along East Way (now concreted) for a couple of hundred yards, then turn right through a metal kissing gate into a field. Walk along the right-hand edge of the field to a stile leading to a footbridge over a small stream. Cross the stream and follow the path between a tumbledown wall and a line of trees on the left and a barbed wire fence on the right. This path can be rather overgrown.

When you reach the road on the edge of Drayton village, cross straight over into a farm track. A short distance from the road, the track swings left and leads through a couple of gates to the churchyard. Walk past the south door of the church to the lych-gate, then turn right along Church Lane. Ignore the path signposted to Sutton Wick on the right by an old pump, and pass the former Methodist Church opposite. Take a footpath through a kissing gate on the right below some horse chestnut trees (just before an old cottage on the left). This path leads over a stile and then across a meadow to another stile at the end of a lane. Walk along this lane, which joins Sutton Wick Lane by the village duck pond. Turn left to reach the Abingdon Road. Cross the road into a bridleway opposite and follow it, slightly downhill at first and then gradually uphill, to the highest point on the walk (a modest 65 metres above sea level). From here you can see Nuneham Courtenay House to the north-east, Faringdon Folly to the west and the Downs to the south, as well as most of Abingdon spread out in front of you.

The bridleway descends (with views of New Cut Mill among the trees) until it reaches a T-junction of tracks. Turn right into a track that immediately bends left. Just before you reach the mill, notice the slightly raised belt of long grass and scrub on the left — this marks the line of the old Wilts and Berks Canal. When you reach the mill buildings, turn right along a lane. The River Ock flows alongside this lane on the left, with the line of the canal again visible as a scrubby bank in the field on the right. New Cut Mill was formerly known as Buggs Mill; it gained its new name when the Ock was realigned when the canal was constructed.

When you reach a footbridge over the Ock on the left (signposted River Ock Walk), cross it and follow the path along the opposite bank, with the Tesco superstore across the fields. The path leaves the river briefly to skirt a small riverside copse then returns to it by a small weir. Just beyond the weir, cross back to the southern bank of the river, then follow a side-stream to another bridge by a children's play area. Walk across past the play area to a path which leads eastwards along a hedge that separates it from the gardens of the houses on the right. After about quarter of a mile, this path leads back to the Drayton Road.

Cross the road to the gate opposite, then take the path on the left that leads to a bridge back over the Ock. Follow this attractive path between the two strands of the river. After a few hundred yards, you cross a bridge over a weir (often dry)

KEY

- `----` FOOTPATH
- `====` TRACK
- `═══` METALLED ROAD
- `≡≡≡` MAJOR ROAD
- `≈≈≈` RIVER
- `+` CHURCH
- `□` BUILDING
- `○` ROUTE OF WALK
- `◇` PUBLIC HOUSE
- `✳` START POINT OF WALK
- `⊜` LAKE OR POND

PUB DETAILS

THE START POINT PUBLIC HOUSE IS THE GEORGE & DRAGON AT SUTTON COURTENAY.

OTHER PUB FEATURED:-

THE OLD ANCHOR INN AT ABINGDON.

NOTE

THIS MAP IS DIAGRAMMATIC ONLY AND IS NOT TO SCALE.

between the two streams; a similar distance beyond this you reach a second bridge over another weir at the confluence of the two streams. Cross the end of the cul-de-sac to a path which leads past a grassy area surrounded by houses, then alongside the churchyard wall to West St. Helen Street. The main route crosses the junction and turns left along East St. Helen Street, but a short (and highly recommended) diversion around the churchyard is as follows. Turn right then immediately right again through the Elizabethen gateway into the churchyard. Walk past Twitty's Almshouses on the right, then turn left in front of Long Alley Almshouses to St. Helen's Wharf. Turn right to visit The Old Anchor Inn and the bridge over the Ock, then turn around. Follow St. Helen's Wharf back past the pub around the east end of the church to return to the junction of East and West St. Helen Street.

Follow East St. Helen Street (signposted County Hall and Museum). When you emerge in the Market Place behind the County Hall, cross Bridge Street at the traffic island. Take a few steps to the left, then turn right and pass under the Abbey Gateway. Walk down Abbey Close (straight ahead) for a little way, then turn right into Checker Walk. This leads to a small car park by the entrance to the Abbey Buildings. Walk through the passageway by the Checker to emerge in Thames Street. Turn right, past the entrance to the Upper Reaches Hotel, to reach Bridge Street opposite the entrance to the Old Gaol. Turn left and cross Abingdon Bridge. You can avoid crossing the busy main road by keeping to the left-hand pavement past the Nag's Head pub and then, once you have crossed the main river channel, taking a flight of steps down to the left and passing *under* the bridge. Walk along the towpath with the Old Gaol and St. Helen's church on the opposite bank. Keep along the river through several gates and stiles, past the entrance to Abingdon Marina on the far bank, until you reach the footbridge over Swift Ditch. Pause to enjoy the view of the old bridge from the footbridge, then keep on along the Thames.

After about half a mile, the towpath leaves the main river to follow the Culham Cut; along this stretch there are fine views of Culham Manor over the fields on the left. When you reach a footbridge, cross the Cut. Follow the path straight ahead to a stone slab bridge over an overgrown ditch. Keep on past a World War II pill box to reach the main weir at the top of Sutton Pools. Cross the weir and follow a delightful path between the backwaters of Sutton Pools, crossing a couple of smaller weirs on the way. From these weirs, you can look enviously at the beautiful houses on the opposite side of the stream (Lord and Lady Asquith lived at The Wharf, the brick and timber cottage closest to the water's edge). All too soon, the path swings to the right over a bridge (a paper mill once stood here) and returns you to Church Street in Sutton Courtenay. Turn right past the cottages to return to your car at the village green.

To the Downs from Blewbury and the Astons

WALK 9
At least 4 hours
7 ½ miles
Walk begins page 56

Background to the Walk

The idea of a downland walk is an idyllic one. Too often, however, reality turns out to be a hard slog through enormous and featureless fields of crops. This walk shows the Downs at their best — fine scenery with extensive views, plenty of historical interest and a profusion of flora and fauna. The route makes use of a variety of easy paths — grassy gallops, village by-ways, chalky tracks and sunken footpaths.

Long stretches of the route are lined with flowers such as Pyramidal and Spotted Orchids, Cowslips, Wild Arum, Horseshoe and Tufted Vetch, and Wild Thyme. These attract a number of species of butterflies. Probably the most noticeable is the Marbled White, which looks a little like a tiny flying chessboard. Other species include Chalkhill and Small Blue, and various Skippers. Bird life is also prolific. In summer, if you are lucky, you may hear the 'wet-my-lips' call of the Quail. You are unlikely to see this species, but other game birds are less secretive (and much commoner)—Pheasant, Grey Partridge and Red-legged Partridge are all widespread in this area. In winter, various waders and birds of prey are occasionally seen. However, the species that epitomises this rolling farmland is the Corn Bunting, a bulky, nondescript bird, which is often seen perched on track-side trees and wires. Its call is said to resemble the jangling of keys. The area around the old rifle range at Churn has turned up a number of rarities — most recently, in 1992, a Woodchat Shrike.

The Downs are also renowned for their archaeological interest, and the area around Blewbury is no exception. Near the rifle range is an impressive pair of round

Maps
Landranger 1:50,000
Sheet 174
Pathfinder 1:25,000
Sheet 1155 (SU 48/58)
Map Reference of Start/
Finish SU530857

How to get there
Blewbury is on the A417
Reading-Wantage road. If you
are approaching on the A34,
leave at the Milton turn;
follow signs to Wantage
(ignore the turning to
Steventon), then turn left at
the Rowstock roundabout.
Drive through the villages of
Harwell and Upton. When
you reach Blewbury, turn into
a no-through road called
Nottingham Fee in the centre
of the village (there is a small
war memorial on the triangle
at the junction with the main
road). The Red Lion is about
150 yards down on the left.
Blewbury is served by two
fairly infrequent bus services
from Didcot: Chiltern Queens
route C (tel. 0491 680354)
and Martins Coaches route 3
(tel. 0494 711298).

Pub facilities
Red Lion, Blewbury
A cosy, old-timbered country
pub which has recently been
refurbished. It has a pleasant
and fairly large garden shaded

by apple trees. The former restaurant is now a non-smoking family room (except when booked for functions), with ramp access for wheelchairs. There is also a toilet for the disabled. The main bar retains its old-fashioned character, with a selection of prints and old photographs on the wall. The landlord has documentary evidence of the building's existence in 1785, but the pub probably dates back to 1650. The pub is the westernmost outpost of the Brakspear's 'empire', based in Henley-on-Thames. Their Old Ale is served all year round (it is usually considered a winter ale), as are their Special and 'ordinary' bitters (the latter is a favourite of the beer writer Michael Jackson and Rumpole's creator John Mortimer). As well as the beers, up to 30 wines are sold by the bottle, with 5 or 6 available by the glass. The Red Lion's food is based on traditional Victorian country cooking, with the emphasis on fresh ingredients (especially fish). Typical menu items include fresh trout fillets with new potatoes, or lamb chop in home-made honey and cider sauce. Vegetarian dishes, and old-fashioned desserts such as apple pie and ginger crumble, are available. Children are welcome in the family room or in the garden; dogs are permitted in the garden only. Walkers in boots are asked to restrict themselves to the main bar. Access, Visa, American Express and Diners Club cards are accepted. Please check with the landlord if you wish to leave your car in the car park while you walk. Tel. 0235 850403.

The model railway in a garden above Aston Tirrold

barrows. For a short while, the route follows the Ridgeway long-distance path, an ancient highway; a little later it crosses another linear ancient monument, the enigmatic Grim's Ditch. Between Aston Upthorpe and Blewbury the path runs below Blewburton Hill, a hill fort founded around 350BC and sporadically occupied until it was apparently sacked in the 1st century AD. Most of the earthworks now visible are thought to have been agricultural rather than military, although the fort has been suggested as a possible site for the Battle of Ashdown in 871, at which Ethelred defeated the Danes.

Churn rifle range has been closed for some years, and is now used by Reading University for field studies. Before World War I, soldiers came here by train on the Didcot-Southampton line (now dismantled). A grassy bank marks the platform of Churn Halt across the field opposite the hut. You may thus be forgiven for

The Red Lion at Blewbury

jumping to ghostly conclusions if you hear a distant whistle a few miles further on. In fact, it will have come from the garden of an isolated bungalow, where the occupier has built a circular track on which he runs miniature replica GWR locomotives, powered by coal. He told me that his engines use about 5 cwt. of coal a season and that he has a problem with the piped water supply, which is hard and quickly furs up the boilers. He intends to solve this by piping rainwater to the tower by the track. We were lucky enough to be invited to join him for a turn around the track, but do respect his privacy (and his geese!) if the trains are not running.

The villages en route live up to the high standard set by the rest of the walk. The 'Siamese villages' of Aston Upthorpe and Aston Tirrold are full of fine cottages. The famous racing stud at Aston Upthorpe is owned by Sheik Ahmed of the Maktoum family. *Mtoto*, winner of the Eclipse Stakes in 1987 and 1988 and the King George at Ascot, was trained here. The stud sponsors the Yorkshire Oaks.

Aston Tirrold United Reformed Church is said to have been founded as an Independent Chapel in 1670 (remarkable if true, since Nonconformism was still illegal at this time). Blewbury is a delightful labyrinth of winding lanes, walled alleyways and stream-side paths among half-timbered and thatched cottages. It is perhaps most famous for its thatched walls, which are seen to advantage in the last hundred yards of the walk. These are built of cob, a mixture of mud, clay and straw, sometimes tempered with horse hair and dung. The cob is laid on a brick or rubble foundation; building these walls must have been a time-consuming process, as each course must be allowed to dry before the next is added. The thatch serves to protect the cob from the effects of rain, though the walls do require a fair amount of maintenance — the wall near the Red Lion was restored in 1993. The whitewashed walls impart a strange medieval-cum-Mediterranean feel to this part of the village. Blewbury will more than repay an extended exploration before or after the main walk, although the described route does give a flavour of its special atmosphere.

Walk 9

Distance: *Allow at least four hours for this downland walk of seven-and-a-half miles.* From the Red Lion, turn right and walk up Chapel Lane and Nottingham Fee towards the main road. Look out for the thatch rats on the roof of one of the cottages! Cross the main road carefully and take the signposted public footpath opposite. Ignore the path leading away to the right, taking instead the wooded path straight ahead. This quickly begins to climb and develops into an attractive hollow way, with flower-laden banks and views over Didcot and Blewbury to Wittenham Clumps (see Walk 10) and Blewburton Hill behind you. After a few hundred yards, you pass the gates of a small covered reservoir on the left — even this is carpeted with flowers — then a similar distance farther on you skirt a small wood which fills the head of a downland combe, also on the left. Shortly beyond this wood, you meet up with a metalled track. Follow it straight ahead.

About 300 yards on, you reach the corner of a small conifer plantation just before the buildings of Upper Chance Farm. A number of paths fan out from this point. Follow a wide grassy gallop that runs just to the right of a second conifer plantation some distance away. To confirm you have chosen the right way, look out for a circular trotting ring in the scrubby grass to the right of the path before you reach the second wood. The path runs along the right-hand edge of this second wood then, at the end of the wood, turns slightly right, away from the gallop you have been following. This path leads just to the right of the trees near the building ahead (the old rifle range hut, now used as a Field Centre) and to the left of two prominent tumuli or burial mounds. You reach a concrete track where a sign (marked Blewbury 2) points back the way you have come.

Cross the concrete track to a grassy track that runs alongside it and turn left past the rifle range hut. Ignore a path that leads off to the right towards a bridge over the disused railway. Follow the wide grassy track straight on, which leads after about quarter of a mile to the Ridgeway. Turn left up the hill. Leave the Ridgeway at a fork, taking a similar track (signposted Public Right of Way) on the left. Ahead of you and slightly to the right, the land rises to Lowbury Hill (610 ft). After about a third of a mile, level with a small wood on the right, a path crosses at right angles. The left-hand turn leads back to Blewbury, 2 miles away, and is a useful short cut if the weather turns nasty. Otherwise, keep straight on.

KEY

- - - - - FOOTPATH
====== TRACK
———— METALLED ROAD
———— MAJOR ROAD
〜〜〜 STREAM
✝ CHURCH
▫ BUILDING
➝ ROUTE OF WALK
○ PUBLIC HOUSE
✳ START POINT OF WALK
||||| HILL FEATURE

Walk 9

NOTE
THIS MAP IS DIAGRAMMATIC
ONLY AND IS NOT TO SCALE

PUB DETAILS
THE START POINT PUBLIC
HOUSE IS THE RED LION AT
BLEWBURY

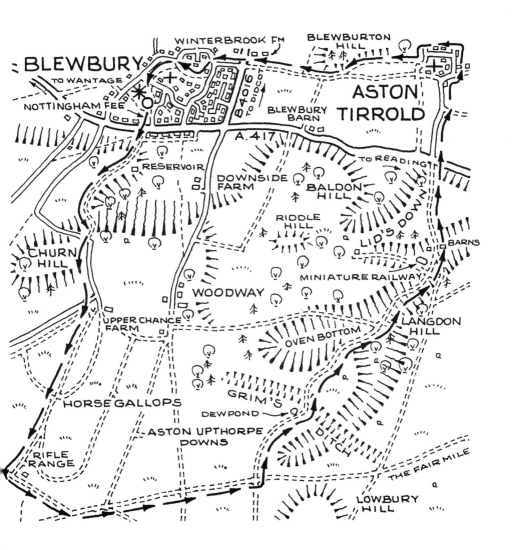

At the foot of Lowbury Hill, just before the track acquires a hedge on its left-hand side, turn left (a small sign on the fence here reads 'Right of Way'). There are views for about 270° from this point. The path, indistinct at first, turns into a fenced track then curves gently rightwards with a scrubby valley down to the right. About half a mile from Lowbury Hill you pass a rare survival on the left: a dewpond, surrounded by trees. It is often almost dry, but is still damp enough to support a small willow or two and a clump of reeds. Grim's Ditch crosses the path just here. The path leads down, more steeply now, to the foot of the wooded slope of Langdon Hill. This part of the walk is very attractive — look out on the left-hand bank for the bright, plain purple flowers of Pyramidal Orchid. Near the end of the wood, notice the model railway in the garden of the bungalow on the left.

Beyond the bungalow, keep left at a barn along a metalled track, with views to Cholsey and beyond to the right. This lane leads for just over half a mile up and then down to the main road. Cross quickly but carefully into Spring Lane opposite, and walk down into Aston Upthorpe, passing the attractive brick buildings of Copse Stile Farm on the right. The road bends sharply to the right then to the left (ignore the footpath that leaves the road at the first bend). Walk past the United Reformed Church on the right, then turn left into Thorpe Street. Pass a fine, newly restored timbered cottage on the right.

Where the street turns sharp right, take a bridleway on the left just beyond the church. This bends right between converted farm buildings, then swings left. At this point, climb a flight of steps to a stile to your right. The path continues parallel to a fence. Blewburton Hill, wooded at this point, rises to the right and the scalloped slope of Lid's Down is visible beyond the main road on the left. The field you are walking in begins to narrow; take a stile on the left to join a bridleway. Turn right, as the earthworks of the hill fort come into view on the right. Stiles allow access to the top, if you can summon up the energy so late in the walk. Otherwise, keep along the bridleway for half a mile to Winterbrook Farm and so to the B4016 on the edge of Blewbury.

Cross straight over into Besselslea Road, and follow it past the entrance to Bridus Mead on the right. When you reach South Street, turn left. After about a hundred yards, take an unsignposted lane on the right by a cottage with a chalk wall. This lane leads past pretty cottages and barns into a shady path by a stream, to emerge in Church End. Turn left into the churchyard, and keep right around the church tower. In the far corner of the churchyard are Bacon's almshouses, two tiny cottages with plaques recording their endowment. In the triangular green beyond, keep left to a footbridge over a small stream. The path then leads between whitewashed cob-and-thatch walls back to the Red Lion and the end of the walk.

A breezy ascent of Wittenham Clumps

WALK 10
Allow 3 ½ hours
5 ¾ miles
Walk begins page 61

Background to the Walk

The twin peaks of Wittenham Clumps are a well-known local beauty spot. Most visitors either drive to the car park just below the top, or walk from Dorchester-on-Thames or Long Wittenham via Little Wittenham. This route avoids the crowds by starting in the attractive and varied village of Brightwell-cum-Sotwell and taking a series of interesting paths up and along the ridge that extends westwards from the Clumps. This ridge runs between the Thames and the Downs, so good views accompany you for almost all the way. The Clumps (also known as the Sinodun Hills) can be seen from many parts of the county. Their status as the number one local landmark has been rather usurped by the nearby cooling towers of Didcot Power Station, but they still loom impressively over the Thames between Shillingford and Little Wittenham, and they still present a stiff climb. The view of Day's Lock, Little Wittenham and Dorchester Abbey from the Clumps is particularly spectacular.

Castle Hill, the more easterly of the two hills, is crowned by an Iron Age hillfort whose banks and ditches are well preserved (and circumnavigated during the course of this walk). The Romans built a villa near Round Hill, and the hillfort on Castle Hill was occupied by Offa, King of Mercia, after he beat Cynwulf of Wessex at the Battle of Benson in 779. Both hills have clumps of trees at their summits, as does Brightwell Barrow, the lesser summit to the east. One of the old beech trees on Castle Hill has a verse carved into its trunk, inscribed by a Joseph Tubb of Warborough around 1844. Although restored in the 1930s, the words

Maps
Landranger 1:50,000
Sheet 164 or 174
Pathfinder 1:25,000
Sheet 1139 (SU 49/59)
Map Reference of Start/
Finish SU582907

How to get there
Brightwell-cum-Sotwell is bypassed by the A4130 between Didcot and Wallingford. Whether you are coming from Didcot or Wallingford, take the first road you see signposted to the village, then keep along The Street to reach the Red Lion. If you miss the correct turning, either of the next two will take you into High Road; take Church Lane and turn left, or Bell Lane and turn right, to reach the pub. The village is served by Chiltern Queens services B, C and K (none of which is particularly frequent — tel. 0491 680354 for further details).

Pub facilities
Red Lion,
Brightwell-cum-Sotwell
(Pictured right)
This pub is reckoned to be almost 500 years old; it may well have incorporated the thatched roof of an even older barn that once stood on the site. It has a cosy beamed interior with an inglenook fireplace and bread oven. Food is competitively priced and the menu typically includes a home-made soup, sandwiches, ploughman's lunches, jacket potatoes, chilli, curries and pasta dishes. Vegetarians are well catered for, as are real ale drinkers as the Red Lion usually serves six real ales at any one time from a range of fourteen. In addition, Beamish stout, Carlsberg and Kronenbourg 1664 lagers and Strongbow and Symond's Scrumpy Jack ciders are available on draught. Parking is limited at the pub, but there is ample street parking and a car park is also available at the recreation ground nearby in Mackney Lane.
Tel. 0491 837373.

of the poem are now hard to decipher — they tell the history of the area and can be read in Little Wittenham Nature Reserve's publication *Our First Ten Years*.

The Reserve is owned and managed by the Northmoor Trust, based at Little Wittenham Manor. The Trust outbid a shooting syndicate to buy Little Wittenham Wood in 1982, and the reserve has since been extended to include the Clumps and the meadow above Little Wittenham. Public access is generally permitted (in return the Trust receives an annual payment of one red rose from the County Council — rather more romantic than the usual 'peppercorn'!). The grassy hills are a good hunting ground for botanists and lepidopterists. Botanical specialities include the rare Loddon Lily, which grows near the river, and grassland plants such as Clustered Bellflower and Harebell. The list of insects recorded includes 474 moth species and 32 butterflies, including Marbled White and Brown Argus. Also frequently to be seen on the wing around the Clumps are model aircraft and kites flown by buffs and children alike, and in snowy weather the steep slopes are a favourite venue for sledging and even skiing at times. The reserve is carefully managed for wildlife — perhaps the most obvious signs of this management within the wooded areas are the ponds that have been dug. These support populations of dragonflies and amphibians, including thousands of toads and one of the largest populations in the country of the rare Great Crested Newt. In addition to the two public rights of way through the woods, there are a number of permitted paths. However, some parts of the wood are kept for wildlife and for research and public access to these areas is restricted.

Brightwell and Sotwell were once separate villages, but were united in 1948. Before this, according to the New Oxfordshire Village Book, a farcical situation arose whereby the parish clerk of Brightwell would write letters to himself in his alternative capacity as parish clerk of Sotwell! The church at Brightwell has a Norman south doorway and an 18th-century brick tower. Behind the church is Brightwell Manor, a Georgian building on the site of an earlier castle, the moat of which is still visible. In a lane named Wellsprings and overlooked by a pretty cottage is the Sat or Sot Well, a spring-fed pond that gave Sotwell its name.

A cottage called Mount Vernon, in Bakers Lane, Sotwell, is occupied by the Dr. Edward Bach Centre. Bach was a Harley Street consultant and homeopath, who gave up his practice in 1930 to developed his system of 38 flower remedies for 'every negative state of mind'. For example, Wild Rose is said to be effective against resignation and apathy, Clematis is recommended as an antidote to absent-mindedness, and so on. Dr Bach lived at Mount Vernon for the last two years of his life up to 1936 and collected his healing plants in nearby countryside. He claimed that he could detect the properties of a plant merely by holding his hand over the flower. The remedies are jealously guarded, and the Doctor's work is continues at the Centre, which is open to the public from 1000-1500 (weekdays).

Walk 10

Distance: *Allow three-and-a-half hours for this fairly hilly walk of nearly six miles.*
Walk left from the door of the Red Lion along The Street, which is lined on both sides by cottages of varying styles and periods. Pass the Post Office and Stores on the right, then keep straight on at the war memorial by the entrance to the church. Beyond the village hall the road bends right then left; at the left-hand bend leave the road and follow an unmetalled track straight on (Watermans Lane). This track is lined with trees, including plum and walnut trees. When you reach the main road cross carefully, then turn to the left into a short stretch of the old road. (Before the road was straightened, it turned through a tortuous series of right-angled bends; the original line of the road can easily be seen on the map.) At the end of this short stretch, you meet the road to Long Wittenham at a metal gate.

Turn right along the road for a few yards, then cross a stile on the right by a Scots Pine at the entrance to Highlands Farm. This leads into a sheep paddock which you cross to a stile in the opposite fence (keep dogs on the lead if the paddock is occupied). From this point, head for the far right-hand corner of the next field. With each upward step, the view behind you becomes more extensive. At the top of the field cross a third stile, then head directly up the hill (keeping the trig point at Brightwell Barrow well to the right). At the brow of the hill, approximately level with the Barrow, turn left towards the hillfort on Castle Hill. When you reach a hedge, pass through the gap and turn right along the edge of the field. Turn left in the corner of the field (alongside Wittenham Woods). As you approach the next corner, ignore the permitted path into the Nature Reserve through a gate on your right. Turn left in the corner so that you are climbing directly towards the hillfort.

A path on the right leads to an inviting woodland ride, by which our route continues having circumnavigated the hillfort — you can save half-a-mile or so of walking by leaving the hillfort for another day and by skipping to the next paragraph. Otherwise, keep on up to a stile at the foot of the first defensive bank. Cross this and the next bank to reach the comparatively flat area below the summit of Castle Hill, with a clump of trees ahead of you. Having rested and admired the view, walk left (clockwise) around the top of the bank. When you meet a well-trodden path ascending from the car park, turn right into the trees. Keep straight on in the middle of the clump, and look out for the Poem Tree on the right at the far edge of the wood. Beyond the wood, walk straight across to the point at which you entered the hillfort. Retrace your earlier steps downhill, crossing the stile at the bottom of the earthworks then walking down the field edge for a short distance to the stile and gate into Little Wittenham Wood, now on the left.

Cross the stile into the wood and walk down a steepish path along a wide ride. At the bottom of the valley you reach a gravelly track above a pond (patrolled by dragonflies). Walk along the track, which immediately begins to climb again. Midway up the hill, leave the track to take a shady path through the trees on the right. This leads slightly downhill to a bridleway near the edge of the wood. Turn right, back into the wood. This bridleway leads straight and level for half a mile through the wood. At the far end, you emerge into fields.

Keep straight on alongside a hedge, passing the remains of Lowerhill Farm at the end of the first field. The track continues in approximately the same direction and is joined by a bridleway from the right. This marks the line of a Roman road from Silchester via Dorchester to Alcester (near Bicester), which is also briefly encountered during Walks 12 and 17. A short distance beyond the buildings of North Farm (where bed and breakfast is available), the track divides into three; take the tree-lined path uphill to the right. At the top of the field, this path bends left then right. From the second bend there is an attractive view of the Thames at Shillingford. The path now leads across open fields to an old apple tree on the site of Sotwell Hill Barn. Take the fenced path straight on (to the right of the trees). This path may be a little overgrown but should present no real problems. To the left is an orchard; again a number of plum trees line the path. The path develops into a hollow way as it leads downhill towards the main road, onto which it emerges near Sheards Garden Centre and Farm Shop. Cross the road carefully and turn right, again using the old main road. Turn left at the entrance to Moreton House, then keep straight on along a hedged path beyond the entrance to the house. This leads to Bakers Lane by the Bach Centre. Turn right along the lane, passing the entrance to Datchet Green on the right. When you reach Bell Lane, turn left and then right into Wellsprings. This leads past some cottages to the Sot Well. Immediately beyond the pond, turn left along a path which leads alongside its outlet, then crosses to the left-hand side of the stream by a bridge made of railway sleepers. The path then follows the stream back to the starting point.

KEY

- - - - FOOTPATH
===== TRACK
≡≡≡ METALLED ROAD
MAJOR ROAD
≋ RIVER
☐ BUILDING
✝ CHURCH
ROUTE OF WALK
PUBLIC HOUSE
START POINT OF WALK
LAKE OR POND
HILL FEATURE

Walk 10

PUB DETAILS

THE START POINT PUBLIC
HOUSE IS THE RED LION
AT BRIGHTWELL CUM
SOTWELL.

NOTE

THIS MAP IS DIAGRAMMATIC
ONLY AND IS NOT TO SCALE.

LITTLE WITTENHAM

RIVER THAME

TO LONG WITTENHAM

RIVER THAMES

OXFORD READING A.423

SHILLINGFORD

LITTLE WITTENHAM WOOD

RUIN

SHILLINGFORD FM

WITTENHAM CLUMPS

FELMORE COPSE

NORTH FARM

CASTLE HILL

BRIGHTWELL BARROW

TO APPLEFORD

REDGATE FM.

HIGHLANDS FARM

A4130 TO DIDCOT

SOTWELL HILL

A4130 TO WALLINGFORD

ISLAND FARM

BRIGHTWELL CUM SOTWELL

TO NORTH MORETON

BRIGHTWELL MANOR

The 'dreaming spires' from wooded Boars Hill

Maps
Landranger 1:50,000
Sheet 164
Pathfinder 1:25,000
Sheet 1116 (SP 40/50)
Map Reference of Start/
Finish SP490015

How to get there
From the Hinksey Hill
roundabout (near Kennington
on the A34 south-west of
Oxford), take the unclassified
road up Hinksey Hill (away
from Oxford). At the top of the
hill, about half a mile from the
roundabout, turn right. Keep
left at the Old Golf Course.
The Fox is on your right just
as the road begins to descend.
From the south-west, Boars
Hill is signposted from the
B4017 between Abingdon and
Cumnor. There is a bus stop
right outside the pub, served
several times a day by Oxford
Bus Company services 44
and 45.

Background to the Walk

Boars Hill is a hilly area south-west of Oxford. Predominantly wooded, it is known for its views of Oxford, for its literary associations, and locally for the wealth of many of its inhabitants. This walk gives a taste of all three, offering wide views from several points, skirting a local nature reserve named in honour of poet Matthew Arnold, and following secretive footpaths that give glimpses of the large houses and their wooded gardens.

Boars Hill has a typical deciduous woodland fauna and flora. The Snowdrops and Primroses of spring are superseded by Foxgloves and Red Campion in the summer. Later in the year, some of the fungi are just as showy, notably the familiar red and white-spotted Fly Agaric. Common woodland birds include Great Spotted Woodpecker, Coal Tit, Goldcrest, Long-tailed Tit and Jay; rarer species like Hawfinch and Lesser Spotted Woodpecker are present but seldom seen. The woods also harbour squirrels, foxes, badgers and various species of deer.

The centrepiece of the walk is Jarn Mound. Although not quite the highest point on the Hill, it was purchased by the Oxford Preservation Trust to preserve the view over Oxford. In 1928-31 the archaeologist Sir Arthur Evans (famous for his excavations at Knossos in Crete) enhanced the views by raising a 50-foot mound. On top of the mound is a dial-plate showing the main landmarks. Since it was raised, the views have been rather reduced by the growth of the surrounding trees (much better views are to be had elsewhere on this route), but the climb up the steep and

Pub facilities
Fox, Boars Hill
(Pictured left)
Stagecoaches from Oxford to
Faringdon used to stop at the
Fox to change horses — the
modern-day kitchen is housed
in the former stable. It is an
interesting pub, with a motto
('Life loves no lookers-on at
this great game') above the
door, framed poetry on the
walls, a vast collection of
business cards tacked to its
beams, and a number of
stuffed animals in glass cases.
A wood-burning stove may be
a welcoming sight in the
winter. In better weather, the
sloping garden alongside a
wood has a good view and on
dry weekends in summer a
barbecue is lit. The pub menu
is changeable but always
wide-ranging, with starters
(such as broccoli and stilton
soup), snacks (jacket potatoes,
burgers, 'ploughperson's
lunches', etc.) and main meals
(lasagne, liver and bacon, pan-
fried trout with prawns and
melted cheese) on offer. Meals
can be paid for by cheque
(with banker's card), Access
or Visa. Three real ales are
usually available, including
Greenall's Original and a
guest beer such as
Wadworth's 6X. There is a
family room and a non-
smoking area inside the pub,
and children's play equipment
in the garden. Dogs are not
allowed inside the bar, but are
welcome in the garden if kept
on leads. As usual, you are
asked to check with the bar
staff if you want to leave your
car at the pub while you walk.
Tel. 0865 735131.

uneven steps to the top is still worth the effort. Sir Arthur also created a wild garden of British plants around the foot of the mound, importing different soils from around the country to support species that otherwise would not grow here. Some of these can still be seen, as can the remains of his rock gardens and artificially created boggy areas and ponds. A memorial to Sir Arthur Evans was erected in 1978 near the entrance to the Mound.

Near Jarn Mound is Matthew Arnold Field, owned by the Oxford Preservation Trust and managed by BBONT as a nature reserve. The area was reputedly given over to allotments tended by Napoleonic prisoners, who dug a well, the site of which is now unknown. Matthew Arnold (1822-88) described the area around Boars Hill in his poems *The Scholar Gypsy* and *Thyrsis*. Other poets who have lived or stayed here include John Masefield, Robert Graves and Robert Bridges.

Sir Arthur Evans lived at Youlbury, now the home of local politician Sir William Goodhart. Part of the estate is given over to a large scout camp. Just above the camp is the highest point on the Hill, hence the siting of the covered Boars Hill reservoir and some masts. There are fine views of Oxford from here. Jan Morris, in her book *Oxford*, describes the experience of this famous view movingly. Particularly prominent (from left to right) are: the copper spire and Cotswold stone tower of Nuffield College; in the central cluster of buildings, the white-painted cupola of the Sheldonian Theatre, the squat dome of the Radcliffe Camera, the spire of St. Mary's Church and the tower of Merton College Chapel; and, to the right and seemingly surrounded by trees, the tower of Magdalen College Chapel. The large white building on the hill behind Oxford, to the left of the Beckley TV mast (see Walk 17), is the John Radcliffe Hospital. At the beginning and end of the walk, there are southerly views over the Vale of White Horse to the Chilterns and the Lambourn Downs.

Much of this walk is through woodland, and the shelter offered by the trees makes this a good choice for a day when the weather is less than perfect. In autumn, the colours of the leaves will add an extra dimension to the walk.

Walk 11

Distance: *Allow a little over two hours for this walk of four-and-a-half miles.*
Leave the car park of the Fox and walk down the road for a few yards. A footpath sign pointing to the right reads — Ramblers Jubilee Circular Walk Footpath. Follow this path down to a small stream, with woodland to the right and views over the Vale of White Horse to the left. Cross the stream by a concrete slab and continue up the opposite slope. By a group of four ash trees outside the forest fence, a path leads right, into the wood. Do not follow it, but keep left along the edge of the field. In the corner, cross a stream via a footbridge with stiles at each end. Head slightly left across the next field: aim for a house chimney above the trees. At the far side of the field, a stile leads into a lane. Turn left for a few yards past a house called Linens Field, then follow a hedged path between the cottages on the right. This leads to a stile into the corner of a paddock. Walk diagonally across to a stile in the wooden fence, then continue in the same direction to the far left-hand corner of the second paddock. Turn left along the hedge and cross the end of a ditch by a double stile. A little way on, cross another double stile through the hedge on the right. This leads along the edge of a narrow field. Just before you reach the end of this field, with houses ahead of you, cross a stile on the right (by a footpath sign) to the other side of the hedge and keep on in the same direction. Pass close to a white-painted house to emerge in Wootton village by a telephone kiosk and post box. Turn right along the road.

After passing Stones Farm on the right and Mayo's Farm on the left, you reach a cottage on the left called Wootton End. Follow the track opposite. This track leads shortly to a gate and stile into a field. Do not enter the field — instead, take a path to the left. This shady path leads attractively along the edge of the wood, passing close to two small ponds in the field on the right. It then climbs to an unusual castellated house. By the entrance to this house, the path joins the end of a lane. A narrow, hedged footpath crosses at right-angles here — take the left-hand turning, right up against the boundary of the garden (and easily overlooked). This path leads down and up through woods to emerge in a flowery meadow owned by the Oxford Preservation Trust. Keep along the left-hand edge of this field, close to a house. In the corner of the field, a stile and staggered gateway lead into a metalled lane. Turn right, passing a post box and the entrance to White Barn. At the top of

KEY

- - - - - - FOOTPATH
===== TRACK
━━━━━ METALLED ROAD
〜〜〜 STREAM
✝ CHURCH
▫ BUILDING
━━▶ ROUTE OF WALK
○ PUBLIC HOUSE
✳ START POINT OF WALK
🪨 LAKE OR POND
⑊⑊⑊⑊ HILL FEATURE

Walk 11

NOTE

THIS MAP IS
DIAGRAMMATIC ONLY
AND IS NOT TO SCALE

PUB DETAILS

THE START POINT
PUBLIC HOUSE IS THE
FOX AT BOARS HILL

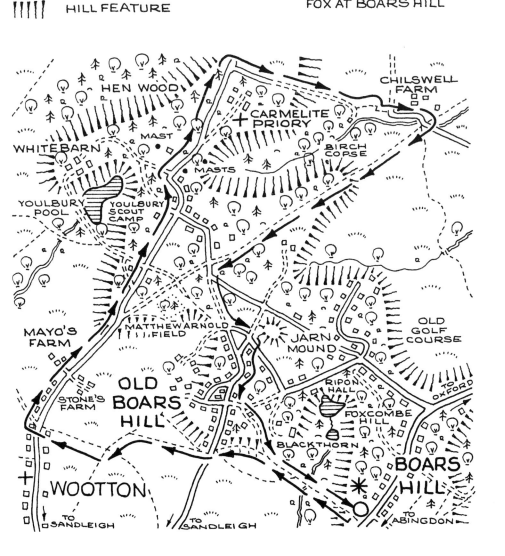

The view of Oxford from Boars Hill

this lane, take the metalled road opposite (not into the scout camp), indicated by a Ramblers Jubilee signpost and a sign to the Carmelite Priory. This road bends left and right around the Boars Hill Reservoir and Pumping Station and the transmitter masts. At the entrance to the Carmelite Priory on the right-hand side, keep along the road to the left. Just past the Priory buildings, the road bends slightly left. Here take a gravelly track on the right. This leads to a field gate with an excellent view of Oxford. Dead ahead, you can also see the Norman tower of Iffley church amongst the trees (see Walk 14), with the Chiltern escarpment behind in the distance.

Beyond the gate, follow the descending track through a field until it bends to the right at the entrance to Birch Copse House. Here, leave the track for a signposted path to the left which skirts the grounds of the House. At the bottom of the field, cross a stile with Chilswell Farm in front of you. Walk around the right-hand edge of the field to reach a bridleway in front of a chalet-style cottage. Go through the farm gate and pass in front of some barns on the left. Just before you reach the farmhouse, take a concrete track on the right, signposted as a bridleway, which immediately bends to the left. Take the first path on the right, over a stile (signposted Redbridge Circular Walk). Walk up the hill to the right of an old dead tree, aiming just left of the point where the line of telegraph wires meets the top of the field. The shrubby slope of the Old Golf Course on Boars Hill is visible away to the left. In the corner of the field at the top is a stile between oak trees. Cross this stile then walk along the left-hand edge of a further field. In the far corner, a path drops into the wood on the left. This path dips quite sharply to a boggy area at the bottom of a hollow, then leads up again though holly bushes and rhododendrons to the rear of a cottage with a pond in the garden. Beyond this cottage the path leads between a brick wall and a line of trees (some of which are only just thicker than the ivy stems they support) past another house to a road. Ignore the path opposite and turn left. After a few yards where the lane bends left, take the first path on the right, to the right of a telegraph pole (*not* through the kissing gate, though this path also leads to Jarn Mound). Bear left after a short distance, through a staggered gate and along the edge of Matthew Arnold Field. Midway along is a bench with a view over the Vale of White Horse to the Downs. When you reach the road, turn left to Jarn Mound. The Mound and Wild Garden are through a kissing gate on the left.

When you have finished looking around the Mound and Garden, start down the lane that leads downhill opposite the kissing gate. Pass a post box on the right, then opposite Orchard Lane take a driveway in front of the thatched Yew Cottage. At a gate marked Hornbeams, keep right. When this drive bends right, our path carries straight on (by a telegraph pole bearing a sign — Ramblers Association Jubilee Walk 1985). This dark and leafy way leads below a series of gardens between rhododendrons, holly and ferns, then emerges suddenly into fields with extensive views. In the middle distance the most noticeable sights are the cooling towers of Didcot Power Station, the spire of St. Helen's Church in Abingdon closer and to the right, and the runways of the former RAF Abingdon (now Dalton Barracks). Turn left and retrace your earlier steps along the wood edge back to the Fox.

From Baldon Green to Nuneham Courtenay

Maps

*Landranger 1:50,000
Sheet 164
Pathfinder 1:25,000
Sheets 1136 (SU 49/59)
& 1116 (SP 40/50)
Map Reference of Start/
Finish SU563993*

How to get there

*From the A4074 Oxford-
Reading trunk road (formerly
the A423), take a turning just
south of Nuneham Courtenay
signposted to the Baldons.
Pass through a gate (usually
open), and shortly afterwards
the Seven Stars is on your
right in the corner of the
village green. Marsh Baldon
can also be reached via Toot
Baldon from the B480, which
is the continuation of the
Cowley Road to the east of
Oxford. Drivers from
Abingdon should take the
A415 towards Dorchester,
then turn left onto the B4015
at Clifton Hampden. At the
Golden Balls roundabout,
turn left; the turning to the
Baldons is on the right after
about three quarters of a mile.
Heyfordian Travel bus 9
passes through the Baldons
twice a week; Nuneham
Courtenay is served by the
hourly 105 Oxford-
Wallingford-Reading service
(operated by Oxford Bus
Company & Reading Buses).*

Background to the Walk

This short walk links the villages of Marsh Baldon, Toot Baldon and Nuneham Courtenay. Toot Baldon and Marsh Baldon are ancient settlements; Nuneham Courtenay is a mere stripling, having been relocated by the first Earl Harcourt in the 18th century.

Although usually considered as two villages nowadays, there are (or have been) a number of Baldons. In addition to the two main villages, Baldon Row (or Bishop's Baldon or Baldon St. Lawrence) is a hamlet near the church of Toot Baldon. Little Baldon, to the south of Marsh Baldon, now exists only as a farm and a handful of modern houses. Toot Baldon was probably the earliest settlement, the others being founded later as the population of the mother village expanded. The various villages and hamlets seem to have been known by different names at different times, and a local rhyme does little to help clarify the confusing situation: 'March Baldon, Toot Baldon/Baldon in between/Big Baldon, Little Baldon/Baldon on the Green.'

The line of a Roman road (also crossed on Walk 10) is followed by the lane to the east of Marsh Baldon village green. This magnificent green is about 24 acres in extent and probably owes its survival to the winter flooding of the stream that runs across the middle, which has deterred building. The church and manor house are sited away from the green — this suggests that when they were founded the green was already surrounded by dwellings, as it is today. Several cottages along the north side of the green were damaged by a fire that occurred during the dry summer of 1866. A hot cinder ignited loose straw that was being used to

Pub facilities
Seven Stars, Marsh Baldon
(Pictured left)
The Seven Stars pub has a superb location overlooking Baldon Green and the cricket pitch. There was once a large pond in front of the pub, but this was filled in during the 1950s. The building was constructed in the 18th century, though it has been restored and extended since. The Seven Stars stocks mainly Morland's beers (Original, Old Masters, Old Speckled Hen and Revival mild), plus Hook Norton Best on draught. Draught lagers are Foster's and Stella Artois, with imported lagers by the bottle. Guinness and Scrumpy Jack cider complete the range of drinks available on draught; there is also a good collection of whiskies. Children are welcome at lunchtimes and early in the evening; there is a good-sized garden and a back room that is often used by families. Although there is usually ample parking on the edges of the green, the landlord will usually allow walkers to use the pub car park, provided they check with him before departing. Opening hours are 1130-1500 and 1900-2300 (Mon-Thurs). On Friday and Saturday evenings the pub opens an hour earlier, and on Sunday normal hours apply. Food is served 1200-1400 and 1900-2130, except on Sunday evenings. Tel. 0867 38255.

rethatch one of the roofs and the fire spread quickly to neighbouring cottages. Its effects might have been less severe if more of the village's menfolk had been on hand to help fight the fire. Unfortunately many of them had taken the long walk to Oxford for St. Giles' Fair. The lack of water probably also hindered attempts to douse the flames as several of the village ponds had dried out. The tiny school building escaped damage. The original school was founded in 1771 at the bequest of one Elizabeth Lane 'for learning to read Six Poor Boys and Six Poor Girls of March Baldon'. The existing schoolroom was built in 1873 (following the Education Act of 1870) and was enlarged in 1896, 1954 and 1991. Water for the school was drawn from a nearby well as recently as the Second World War, when the normal water supply was found to be contaminated. The school celebrated its bicentenary in 1971.

The green was once ringed by no fewer than 14 ponds. Nowadays there are only two or three, but one of the survivors, the school pond, attracted an unusual visitor in the summer of 1960 in the shape of a Red-necked Phalarope. Only six of these rare waders have ever been seen in the county.

The unfenced road across the green runs through the outfield of the cricket pitch — during the season two white-painted lines mark the lane where it crosses the boundary in front of the small pavilion. There cannot be many pitches where incoming batsmen have to 'stop, look and listen' on their way to the crease! Near the pavilion, the 'fine elm' mentioned in the *Victoria County History* of 1954 is little more than a stump, having succumbed to Dutch Elm Disease.

Crown Inn, Toot Baldon (Pictured right)
The Crown had been closed for some time when
the current landlord and landlady moved in
during 1992, and it is good to see a village pub
brought back from extinction. The pub is now
well kept, and the food (cooked by the landlady,
a cordon bleu chef) is very popular — so much
so that you are advised to book in advance if
you intend to eat here (tel. 0867 38240). Food
is not served on Monday evenings. The pub
serves a range of starters, light snacks and
home-cooked specials, all of which are listed on
a blackboard. Main meals include vegetarian
pasta with garlic, mushrooms, cream and
cheese; baked trout with bacon, mushroom and
herbs; and chicken supreme pan-fried with
ginger, lemon, fresh coriander and cream. There
is also a choice of grills and puddings. Draught
ales are Charles Wells' Bombadier, Morland's
Original and Fullers' London Pride. Guinness,
Foster's, Stella Artois and Dry Blackthorn
cider are all available on draught. Walkers may
leave their cars at the pub at their own risk.
Children and dogs are welcome, except in the
main bar area.

The **Harcourt Arms** at **Nuneham Courtenay**
is about three quarters of the way round the
walk; it is a popular main-road pub with a large
restaurant.

Toot Baldon is at the top of a hill ('Toot' comes from the Anglo-Saxon word for
a look-out post). Much of the surrounding land was owned by Queen's College,
and the village was used as a retreat by members of the university in times of
plague and war. Arthur Young, the 19th-century Secretary to the Board of
Agriculture, noted that the land was wet, despite the village's hilltop location. The
water-table is still close to the surface — the cellar of the Crown is kept cool by a
spring. The Manor House nearby is an imposing early 17th-century building. Toot
Baldon church has a Norman doorway, and original 13th-century arcades, and
there is a 15th-century cross in the churchyard. A monument inside the church
honours the memory of 41 men who died in an air crash at Little Baldon in July
1965. In an earlier disaster, some cottages near the church were destroyed and 11
servicemen died when an American aircraft crash-landed in 1945.

Nuneham Courtenay has an interesting history. The old village and church near
the River Thames were demolished in the 1760s by Earl Harcourt so as not to
interrupt the classical vistas from Nuneham House. The famous landscape
gardener Lancelot 'Capability' Brown was engaged in the laying out of the
grounds, though little of his work remains today. Horace Walpole described the
park in 1780 as the most beautiful in the world. The new village with its inn (the
Harcourt Arms) and forge was built in its current position along the main road. It

was suggested that the old village of Nuneham Courtenay was the model for the village of Auburn in Oliver Goldsmith's poem *Deserted Village*, despite the poet's disapproval; to modern eyes the semi-detached brick cottages of the 'new' village are picturesque although uniform in design. The first Earl Harcourt also built the new village church as a landscape feature for the park. It is a rather odd-looking Romanesque building, though its location in fields and near a pond is attractive.

Nuneham Courtenay Arboretum, which is administered by the Botanic Gardens in Oxford, is open every day between May and October. The entrance to the arboretum is on the A4074, just off the route south of the turning to the Baldons.

Marsh Baldon church, near the end of the walk, has an unusual octagonal tower, which was originally intended to carry a spire. It is worth strolling to the rear of the church to take a look at the carved sundial in the south porch. This is believed by some authorities to be Saxon, though Nikolaus Pevsner suggests it is more likely to be 12th century.

Baldon House, next to the church, was the home of Sir Christopher Willoughby, an agricultural reformer. Arthur Young devotes several pages of his *General View of the Agriculture of Oxfordshire* of 1813 to the opinions of various local landowners and farmers on the vexed question as to whether fresh or rotten dung made the better fertiliser; Sir Christopher was a devout supporter of the latter point of view, declaring that dung should be stored in heaps until 'very rotten'. He also recommended the use of pigeon droppings as a dressing for barley. He considered it so beneficial that he believed it was worth keeping a dovecote for the droppings alone, even without the eggs and meat the pigeons also provided. His dovecote can still be seen a short distance along the footpath behind the church.

Walk 12

Distance: *Allow about two hours for this easy walk of just over four miles (which could be divided into two separate short walks of about two miles each).*

Follow a track along the bottom of Marsh Baldon village green from the Seven Stars, starting out past a cottage with a thatch fox and chicken on its roof. This track passes several cottages in a variety of building styles, then curves to the left by Durham Leys Farm, which has a large tree-lined duckpond at its gate. The path then bends right and left, then right again around an attractive thatched cottage by a stream. Behind the cottage, you come to a T-junction; turn right into a track that subsequently curves to the left.

Before the track reaches some farm buildings, take a track that leads off to the left (opposite a bridleway, sometimes badly overgrown, which leads away to the right). The left-hand track leads between fields with a good view on the right to the Chilterns with the churches of Garsington and Cuddesdon on their respective hilltops in the foreground. After a while, the grassy track leads gently downhill to a field corner below Toot Baldon church. At this point, there is a slightly awkward crossing of the two branches of the stream and a hedge. Follow the path up the sloping field to a kissing gate which gives access to the churchyard. Once you have looked around the simple church, leave via the lych-gate and turn right past the end of the church. This drive leads along an avenue of horse chestnut trees, with a pond to the left, to reach the road in Toot Baldon village. Turn right for a few yards to sample the Crown Inn (and, if time permits, to view the manor house down a lane on the left just beyond the pub) then turn back down the road. Keep to the road at the entrance to the avenue to the church. Pass a modern row of houses on the right called Wilmots (named after a 17th-century benefactor of the village) and ignore a bridleway that leads away to the right by New Farm Cattery. Follow the road round to the left then, when it swings to the right, take a metalled no-through road on the left. This lane eventually leads back to Toot Baldon church; however, our route leaves it at the first right turn to follow a tree-shaded byway. This leads down to a small stream then back up to a metalled road, where you keep straight on, past several attractive cottages. Beyond two barns, one on either side of the lane, turn right onto a lane that leads along the northern edge of Marsh Baldon green, passing the school and pond on the way. When you reach the main village road, turn right and walk away from the green, up the lane between cottages and their gardens. A couple of hundred yards beyond the village hall and the last of the houses, the road bends to the right. Take a hedged bridleway on the left (the entrance is blocked to cars by a metal bar). This leads pleasantly through fields for half a mile or so past some old barns and through an avenue of mature trees (mostly oaks). Eventually the chimneys of the estate cottages at Nuneham Courtenay come into view, and the path meets the busy main road. Cross carefully and follow the footpath sign opposite alongside the Harcourt Arms to a stile in the corner of the car park. Cross the field diagonally towards the church; the path passes close to a pond and then crosses a stepless stile into a metalled lane. Turn right, past the church. Walk down the lane for about 200 yards, until a belt of trees joins on the left.

If time permits, you might like to continue along the track for a there-and-back glimpse of Nuneham House and the lake; otherwise, turn left through a (rather tight!) wooden kissing gate. The path leads alongside the belt of trees on its way back towards Nuneham village, crossing a number of stiles as it does so. When you reach the main road once more, cross carefully again. Turn right then immediately left, following the road to the Baldons. This leads through woodland, then past a row of houses and the entrance to Baldon House on the right. Shortly after this, you reach Marsh Baldon church. When we last walked this way, we were amused by a grey squirrel which showed a good deal of road sense by crossing from one side to the other at tree height using the telephone line as a bridge! Pass through the gate between a cottage and the church to return to Marsh Baldon green and the Seven Stars.

If there is a cricket match in progress you may want to enjoy watching a few overs with a glass in your hand as the shadows lengthen on this most English of scenes. Even in the winter it is worth strolling a few yards up the road to view the quaint pavilion, the boundary line on the road and the hollow stump of the elm.

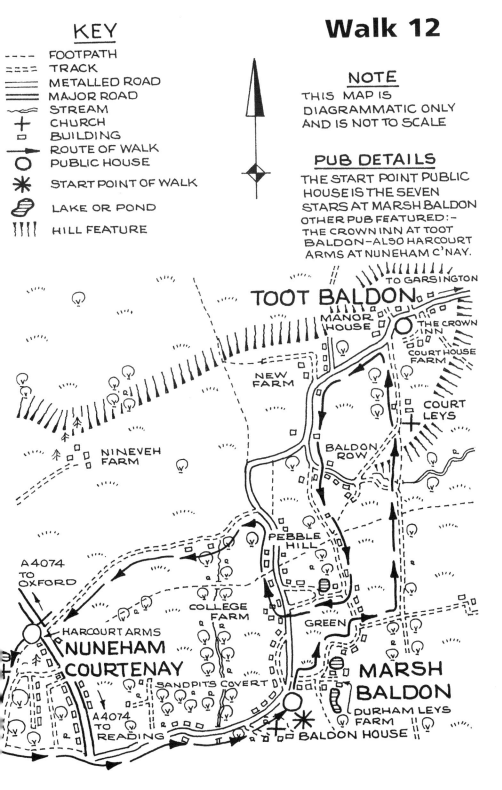

KEY

- ` ---- ` FOOTPATH
- ` ==== ` TRACK
- METALLED ROAD
- MAJOR ROAD
- STREAM
- CHURCH
- BUILDING
- ROUTE OF WALK
- PUBLIC HOUSE
- START POINT OF WALK
- LAKE OR POND
- HILL FEATURE

Walk 12

NOTE

THIS MAP IS DIAGRAMMATIC ONLY AND IS NOT TO SCALE

PUB DETAILS

THE START POINT PUBLIC HOUSE IS THE SEVEN STARS AT MARSH BALDON OTHER PUB FEATURED:– THE CROWN INN AT TOOT BALDON–ALSO HARCOURT ARMS AT NUNEHAM C'NAY.

TO GARSINGTON

TOOT BALDON

MANOR HOUSE

THE CROWN INN

COURT HOUSE FARM

NEW FARM

COURT LEYS

BALDON ROW

NINEVEH FARM

PEBBLE HILL

A4074 TO OXFORD

COLLEGE FARM

GREEN

HARCOURT ARMS

NUNEHAM COURTENAY

SANDPITS COVERT

MARSH BALDON

A4074 TO READING

DURHAM LEYS FARM

BALDON HOUSE

Two 'Great' villages; Milton and Haseley

Maps
Landranger 1:50,000
Sheet 164 or 165
Pathfinder 1:25,000
Sheet 1117 (SP 60/70)
Map Reference of Start/
Finish SP630028

How to get there
From Junction 7 of the M40,
follow the A329 towards
Wallingford. Take the first
turning on the right,
signposted to Great Milton.
The Bull is on the village
green in the centre of the
village. Great Milton can also
be reached by minor roads
from Wheatley and
Cuddesdon, or from Abingdon
via Clifton Hampden,
Stadhampton and Little
Milton. Oxford Bus Company
services 203 (Oxford-Little
Milton, 5 journeys per day)
and 211 (Thame-Chalgrove, 1
journey per day) stop at the
green in Great Milton.

Pub facilities
Bull Inn, Great Milton
The Bull is an eyecatching
thatched building overlooking
the village green. It was built
in the 17th century and has a
beamed interior and an
inglenook fireplace in the
Lounge Bar. There are a
number of old photographs of
the pub on the walls of the
Lounge. The large garden to

Background to the Walk

In the language of estate agents, Great Milton is a 'much sought-after' village. The combination of olde-worlde rural charm and close proximity to the M40 make this prime commuter country; however, the conversation in the public bar of the Bull was on matters agricultural when I last called in. The exclusivity of Great Milton is confirmed by the presence of Le Manoir Aux Quat' Saisons, Raymond Blanc's famous restaurant, at Great Milton Manor. This is one of only five two-starred restaurants in the Michelin Red Guide to Great Britain. The manor was originally built in the 15th century, but has been extended and altered, mainly in the 17th and 20th centuries. The oldest part is closest to the church; the modern entrance is in a wing built in 1908. Facing the road between this entrance and the church is a blocked but imposing 17th-century gateway, originally the main entrance to the manor. In the grounds are a medieval fishpond and dovecote, both older than the house itself.

The name Milton, perhaps surprisingly given the presence of the watermill on the River Thame and several nearby windmill sites, does not come from 'mill town', but from 'middle town'. Persistent local tradition has it that the ancestors of the poet John Milton lived in the Manor House and took their name from the village. It has even been suggested that Milton was fond of visiting his ancestral home. There is little to substantiate either of these stories, though the poet did visit John Thurloe, Secretary of State to Oliver Cromwell, at The Priory. Cromwell himself was another of Thurloe's famous visitors.

The Bull Inn at Great Milton

There are several other buildings of interest in Church Road. The Priory has a fine 16th-century façade and the Boyle coat of arms above the entrance. There has never been a priory here — the name, coined in the 19th century, probably refers to the building's location on the site of a tithe barn of Eynsham Abbey. Just off the green and raised above the road is Priory Bank, a pretty row of 18th-century labourers' cottages. Nearby Romeyn's Court was originally built by Sir Thomas Benger, who was Master of the Revels to Queen Elizabeth I. It was originally a prebendal farm (known as Milton Magna) as was Monkery Farm (Milton Ecclesia), which was associated with Lincoln Cathedral as early as 1146. The current house is partly 15th century, but was restored by Sir John Aubrey in the early 19th century. Finally, the visible parts of the Great House (opposite the church) are mainly of the 18th century, but these conceal an older building.

The church itself is very interesting. It contains an impressive marble monument to Sir Michael Dormer, his wife Jane and his father Sir Ambrose Dormer. On the wall above the tomb are the knight's helmet, sword and chaplet or wreath (worn on the helm). The Dormer seat was at Ascott near Stadhampton; only the gateposts now survive after the house burnt down in 1662. Judging by the scorch marks on stones in one of its walls, the church too suffered a fire (thought to have occurred in the 13th century). In the chancel is a small

the rear has swings and climbing equipment for children, and there are a couple of tables on the narrow lawn in front of the pub from which to view the pleasant village green. Morrell's Varsity and Bitter are available on draught, as are Murphy's and Guinness for stout drinkers (that is to say, drinkers of stout!). Kronenbourg & Harp lagers and Strongbow cider complete the list. In addition, there is a guest beer which changes every couple of months. There is a good selection of home-cooked food on the blackboard (including specials such as Mexican chicken or tagliatelle), plus an à la carte menu with starters and substantial main courses. Light meals include jacket potatoes, ploughman's lunches, salads and sandwiches. Several of these are suitable for vegetarians. A selection of wines is also available. Opening hours are 1100-1430 and 1800-2300 (except Sundays). Food is served until 1400 at lunchtime and 2200 in the evening. Children are welcome in the pub if you are eating (and in the garden if not); keep your dog on a lead and out of the dining area. The usual request to check with the landlord before leaving your car applies. Tel. 0844 279726.

You might also like to visit **The Bell Inn**, *a Free House opposite the Bull — note though that it is closed on Tuesday and Wednesday lunchtimes.* **The Plough** *in* **Great Haseley** *is usefully placed about halfway around the walk.*

recess, said to be an 'acoustic jar' to improve the resonance of the choristers' voices. In a case near the font are some old musical instruments that used to accompany the singers before the church organ was installed. The church was restored by Sir George Gilbert Scott in the middle of the 19th century.

Look out in the churchyard (and also in the churchyard at Great Haseley) for Spotted Flycatchers. These nondescript grey-brown summer visitors seem to find gravestones to be excellent perches from which to launch their sallies in pursuit of flying insects.

Great Haseley is another village of fine stone houses and thatched cottages. The village name, shared with Little Haseley, means simply 'hazel lea'. It too has an imposing church (usually locked, unfortunately) with a number of interesting monuments inside, including the effigies of two knights. One of these is rather worn, but the other shows its subject (Sir William Barrentyne, a London gold-smith) in chain mail, with sword drawn. His helmet and gauntlets are also on display. The west doorway at the foot of the Perpendicular tower is of around 1200, though it is not in its original position. John Leland, the 16th-century antiquary, was awarded the living of Great Haseley by Henry VIII as a reward for visiting the cathedrals, monastic colleges, libraries and record offices of the nation during the compilation of his *Itinerary*. The Reverend Christopher Wren held the living in the 17th century. His son, later to become arguably the most famous architect of all time, was probably educated at Haseley School, founded in 1600.

There is a windmill on a low hill between the village and the main road. The mill was built in the 1760s; a date stone of 1806 probably refers to repairs, as does a date of 1889 on the ironwork inside. The mill ceased working before World War I. It was restored, though not to working condition, in 1975-6. It retains its metal-clad cap and two of its sails and Wilfred Foreman, in his book *Oxfordshire Mills*, states that the interior workings are in 'fair condition'. The foundations of the mill are said to descend for 40 feet beneath the ground, giving the structure a total height of around 100 feet. The stone used to build the mill was quarried nearby; the hollow marking the site of the quarry is known as Mill Dip. There were also windmills at Great Milton and Little Milton, both of which still stood in 1900 but did not survive much longer. The three windmills were part of a series stretching up the eastern side of Oxfordshire from the Chilterns to Otmoor. There are few windmills to the west of Oxford (though one, at North Leigh, survives and can be seen from Walk 20). The location of windmills in the county tended to be determined by local agricultural demand rather than the availability of suitable sites.

The surrounding countryside is fairly undistinguished, but it was doubtless a relief to the villagers when a recent proposal to build a new town nearby (to be called Stone Bassett) was abandoned in the face of local objections.

Walk 13

Distance: *Allow about two hours for this easy stroll of nearly three-and-a-half miles between and around two villages.*

Leave Great Milton village green by way of Church Road (between The Bell and The Bull). Pass Priory Bank, a row of thatched cottages on the left, and keep on past Monkery Farm on the right and The Priory on the left. By the Old Vicarage, the road to Cuddesdon leads off to the right; keep left along Church Road. When you reach the church, keep on past the blocked 17th-century gateway and the automatic gates at the modern entrance to Le Manoir on the left. Shortly afterwards a footpath crosses the road (a gate on the right bears a sign reading Windmill Farm). Turn left along a farm track; when the track bends left into the farm, keep straight on along the left-hand edge of the field. Walk slightly uphill to a stile in the corner of the field. Cross the stile

Great Haseley windmill, built c.1760

then follow a path to the right that leads along the top edge of the field. There are glimpses of the manor and the church through the trees over your right shoulder. This path leads eventually to a wooden gate onto the main road.

Cross carefully and pass through a gap in the fence on the opposite side. Turn left along a stretch of the old road by the last of the buildings of Haseley Industrial Estate. Just past two gas tanks in a small compound, take a path on the right signposted to Great Haseley. This leads along a field edge with views of Great Haseley windmill on the left and to the Chilterns and Wittenham Clumps (see Walk 10) on the right. Didcot Power Station is (somewhat inevitably) visible, and the contrast between the windmill and its modern counterpart is striking. About halfway to Great Haseley the path switches to the right-hand side of the fence, then crosses two fences to reach a perpendicular path below the windmill. Turn right, away from the windmill (the route runs close by later). When you reach a stony track (Back Way) at the edge of Great Haseley, turn left then immediately right down a narrow path. This leads past the back of a cottage, then left to the top of Mill Lane with pretty thatched cottages on all sides. Turn right and walk down to the main street (Rectory Road), then turn left. A short distance on, you see three semi-detached houses arranged in a semicircle on the right with footpaths between each of them. Take the path between the left-hand pair of houses. This leads between gardens to a driveway; follow the path opposite, over the worn remains of a stone stile.

A pretty corner of Great Haseley

The path emerges in a field behind the houses of Great Haseley. Keep along the left-hand edge, up against the rear walls of the gardens. At the end of the field, the path goes by a wisteria-covered cottage to reach a gate into a lane near the church. Unless you intend to visit the church, turn left. At a road junction before a thatched cottage, turn left into the main village street. Walk down past a number of attractive houses, including The Plough, back to Mill Lane. Retrace your steps up the lane, across Back Way and along a field edge. At the crossroads of paths, keep straight on to the windmill. The path passes close to the right of the windmill, then leads past a workshop and along a drive to the main road.

Cross the main road and take the path over a stile opposite. Pass some young trees that have been planted in the field, keeping to the left-hand hedge. At the far side of the field a gate and stile lead out into Thame Road, Great Milton. Turn left and follow the road back to the village green.

Walk 13

KEY

- ---- FOOTPATH
- ==== TRACK
- ═══ METALLED ROAD
- ═══ MAJOR ROAD
- ～～ STREAM
- ✝ CHURCH
- ▫ BUILDING
- → ROUTE OF WALK
- ○ PUBLIC HOUSE
- ✳ START POINT OF WALK
- ▤ LAKE OR POND
- ⁏⁏⁏⁏ HILL FEATURE

NOTE

THIS MAP IS
DIAGRAMMATIC ONLY
AND IS NOT TO SCALE

PUB DETAILS

THE START POINT
PUBLIC HOUSE IS THE
BULL INN AT Gᵀ MILTON

OTHER PUBS FEATURED:-
1. BELL INN, Gᵀ MILTON
2 THE PLOUGH, Gᵀ HASELEY

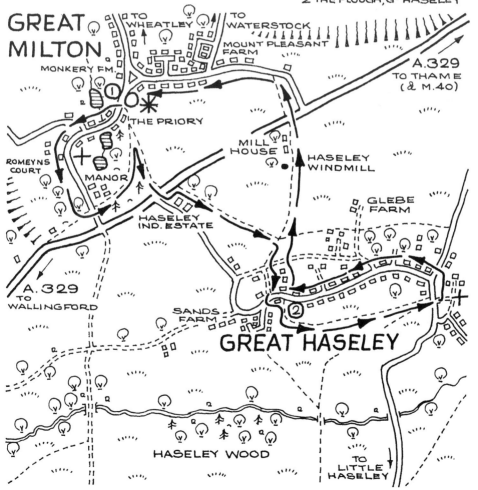

Boathouses and backwaters close to Oxford

Maps
Landranger 1:50,000
Sheet 164
Pathfinder 1:25,000
Sheet 1116 (SP 40/50)
Map Reference of Start/
Finish SP527035

How to get there
Follow the Iffley Road
(A4158) from Oxford, then
take Iffley Turn (signposted to
Iffley). 100 yards later at a
mini-roundabout, turn right
into Church Way. Follow
Church Way for about half a
mile until you see a large
horse chestnut tree in front of
Iffley church. Park
thoughtfully near the church.
The Isis Tavern is about half a
mile away by footpath, and
cannot be reached by car. The
Oxford Bus Company 7A
Nipper Minibus service
terminates near the church;
several routes (including OBC
routes 5, 40, 41, 42 and 43)
serve Iffley Road and Rose
Hill. Several cheap and
frequent bus services run from
the City Centre to Redbridge
Park-and-Ride, an alternative
starting point.

Background to the Walk

Nowhere on this walk are you further than two miles from the centre of Oxford but, for all but a couple of short stretches, the aspect is rural. The route follows intriguing paths through water-meadows, crossing several Thames tributaries as well as the main navigation channel. Many of these paths recall the days when Iffley and South Hinksey were country villages, entirely separate from Oxford. On a modern map, Iffley looks to have been engulfed by the spreading suburbs, but when you get there it is still unmistakably a village — South Hinksey, even now, is set among fields, but the roar of traffic on the nearby Western Bypass is ever-present.

Iffley's most famous building is its Norman church. Sir Nikolaus Pevsner called it 'a magnificent little church... one of the best preserved C12 village churches in England'. It appears on the dust jacket of the Oxford-shire volume of his *The Buildings of England*. The south and west doorways are exuberantly decorated with beakhead, zigzag and sawtooth carving. Take a close look at the capitals (the top parts of the columns) of the south doorway: they represent two horsemen fighting, a centaur suckling her young and Samson and the lion. Most of the fabric of the church dates from the 12th and 13th centuries, although the building was sensitively restored in Victorian times. The horse chestnut tree at the entrance to the churchyard was planted in 1838 to commemorate the opening of the Parochial School in the village; the yew within the churchyard cannot be aged so precisely, but is thought to be over 1000 years old.

The Isis Tavern at Iffley Lock

Pub facilities
Isis Tavern, Iffley
The Isis has an isolated location next to the River Thames just above Iffley Lock. There is no public vehicular access, and beer was still being delivered by punt as recently as 1979. This Morrell's pub is decorated with rowing memorabilia, including oar blades from Boat Race winners, and a whole boat suspended from the ceiling. The riverside garden is popular in the summer, but its secluded position prevents the Isis from getting too busy, even at the height of the tourist season. Out of season, it can be very quiet. Food includes pub staples like chicken Kiev as well as snacks (filled rolls etc.) and vegetarian dishes. Beers served are Morrell's Best and Varsity, plus Graduate or a guest beer. Pimms and lemonade is a popular summertime tipple. A feature of the pub is a rare 19th-century nine-pin skittle alley, which can be booked. Bar billiards, darts and an open fire add to the list of attractions.
Tel. 0865 247006.

Just below the church is Iffley Lock. A mill stood on the eastern bank until it was burned to the ground in 1908, and is commemorated by a millstone and a carved stone plaque. The mill was painted by J. M. W. Turner, and by the watercolourist Peter de Wint (1784-1849). There are two bridges linking the lock with the western bank of the river. The downstream bridge is a replica of the Mathematical Bridge at Queens' College, Cambridge; the stone bridge above it bears a bronze sculpture of a bull's head on its riverward face. This bronze honours Lord Desborough who, in his capacity as Chairman of the Thames Conservancy Board, opened the remodelled lock in 1924. The bull's nose once held a ring, to which the starting rope for bumping races was attached.

Iffley Meadows, which surround the Isis Tavern, are an SSSI (Site of Special Scientific Interest). Leased to the local naturalists' trust BBONT by Oxford City Council, this is one of the few places where the Snakeshead Fritillary still grows wild. The fritillaries flower in April and May, though in small numbers. They were once much more plentiful, and were picked by the armful and sold in Oxford; they were also used for May Day garlands. (An aside in *Companion into Oxfordshire* reveals the unenlightened attitudes of the day towards nature conservation: 'even the lock-keeper's son, with the dual advantage of local knowledge and early rising, was only able to discover two miserable specimens; the only fritillaries picked in Iffley in 1933.') Another interesting plant that grows here is Adder's-tongue, an indicator of land that has not been damaged by agriculture. The meadows are flooded in most winters.

South Hinksey has several pretty cottages, and a 13th-century church with a Georgian chancel. The round-headed Georgian windows are seen to advantage from the road, but the church is usually locked. The General Eliott pub commemorates a former Governor of Gibraltar who was awarded the Freedom of the City of Oxford in 1787.

The surfaced path from South Hinksey to the railway has numerous footbridges. It is known as The Devil's Backbone, presumably because of its raised appearance and some sinuous curves where it crosses the Hinksey Stream. This backwater of the Thames leaves the Seacourt Stream near North Hinksey and rejoins the main Thames channel just north of Kennington. The lake on the other side of the railway, in common with many track-side pools, was formed when gravel was extracted for the railway. It is marked on an 1840s edition of the Ordnance Survey

Iffley Church

map, before most of the houses that now surround it had been built. Nearby in Hinksey Park is a model boating lake and an outdoor swimming pool.

Abingdon Road was once a great causeway; Eastwyke Farm (now a farm shop) gains a mention in Pevsner 'only because it is a farmhouse' (with sheep grazing) just over a quarter of an hour's walk from Christ Church'. That was in 1974; the sheep are now largely gone, though Iffley Meadows are grazed in autumn as part of BBONT's management programme. The stone-built farmhouse is picturesque nonetheless.

Rowing is an almost constant theme of this walk. You may well see college eights in training on the river; the Isis Tavern is decorated with rowing memorabilia, and is often visited by crews after training. At South Hinksey the route passes the workshop of an 'Oar, Scull and Mast Specialist' opposite the church; behind Eastwyke Farm you will often see boat trailers. The college boathouses make an interesting picture on the far side of the river — the atmospheric opening scene of the *Inspector Morse* episode *The Secret of Bay 5B* was shot near this point. Beside the last of the college boathouses, the River Cherwell enters the Thames. The natural course of the Cherwell enters a little way upstream *against* the current of the Thames, which caused the waters to back up and flood Christ Church Meadow; the artificial cut you see here was dug in 1884 to prevent this. Near the end of the walk, Donnington Bridge (opened by Viscount Hailsham in 1962) is often 'decorated' with triumphal graffiti painted by victorious crews.

Walk 14

Distance: *Allow just over two hours for this interesting walk of four-and-a-half miles.* The walking is easy and much of it is on surfaced tracks and paths — however, after prolonged rain, the low-lying water-meadows below Iffley may be flooded. Please note that the path from Abingdon Road to the Thames at Eastwyke Farm is a permitted path and is closed after 4 pm in winter and 9 pm in summer. A diversion is described below if the path is not available.

From the entrance to Iffley churchyard, walk down Mill Lane. The lane bends to the right; shortly after the bend, take a metalled footpath on the left signposted to Iffley Lock. When you reach the river, notice the remains of the mill on the left of the path, then cross a couple of roofed weir-bridges to reach the lock. Cross the downstream lock gate, then use either of the two bridges to reach the towpath on the western bank. Turn right (upstream) along the towpath, reaching the Isis Tavern after a few yards.

Beyond the pub and the boathouse of Oxford Brookes University (formerly Oxford Polytechnic), cross a stile into Iffley Meadows on the left. A right-of-way leads diagonally across the BBONT reserve, but if the growth is lush or the ground wet, walk around the right-hand edges of the field. Near the far corner, a bridge crosses a ditch; in the next meadow, head half-left to a gate. This leads to a footbridge over a backwater, a couple of small weirs and a second footbridge. An old cottage stands above the weir pool and a group of picturesque houseboats make for a colourful scene. The path emerges into the busy Weirs Lane, the continuation of Donnington Bridge Road. Turn left, then left again into Canning Crescent. This curves round, past St. Luke's Church on the right, to meet the Abingdon Road.

Turn left past the milestone (Abingdon 5 miles) on the pavement. Cross the Abingdon Road in front of the Rivermead Rehabilitation Centre and take the road towards the railway bridge, passing the end of Bertie Place on the right and a car showroom on the left. There is a large camping shop (with a campsite) opposite the Redbridge Park-and-Ride car park. Cross the Hinksey Stream and the railway bridge, then leave the road on a track to the right by a bus stop (opposite the end of Kennington Road on the left).

This track immediately curves round to the right. On the bend, take a footpath leading straight on. This path is sometimes overgrown and is easily overlooked — if you pass the concrete posts of an old hut to the right of the track, you have gone too far. The path leads through some bushes to a stile over a fence, and into a meadow. Walk parallel to the nearest line of pylons until you reach a stile and a bridge over a stream (the source of this stream, in a wood above Chilswell Farm on Boars Hill, is passed on Walk 11). Cross another stile on the left to a path leading alongside a hedge, then negotiate a further stile into a narrow belt of trees. At the end of the trees, yet another stile leads into the corner of a field; walk along the right-hand edge with the tower of

The Mathematical Bridge at Iffley Lock

South Hinksey church ahead of you. In the far corner of the field, cross a stile into a stony lane (Barleycott Lane) and turn left.

When you reach St. Lawrence Road, turn right and pass the church. Walk round right- and left-hand bends, passing some attractive cottages on both sides. At Horseshoe Cottage, turn right (signposted Public Footpath) past the Village Hall and the General Eliott pub. When you reach a field gate beyond the pub, keep left along a tarmac path, The Devil's Backbone. This leads under a line of pylons and over the Hinksey Stream to the railway footbridge. From the railway bridge, you can see Old Tom Tower (the upper parts built by Sir Christopher Wren), the rotunda and spire of All Saints' Church (now the library of Lincoln College), the dome of the Radcliffe Camera and the squat spire of Christ Church Cathedral.

At the foot of the steps beyond the railway, another bridge spans a lake (look out for Great Crested Grebes in summer and other wildfowl in winter). When you return to dry land, turn left to emerge at the end of Lake Street. Walk right along Lake Street, passing two pubs, to Abingdon Road. Turn left to a traffic island in front of Hinksey Park and cross over. Take a few steps back the way you came, then turn left down the lane alongside the wall of Eastwyke Farm. (If this path is closed, walk along Abingdon Road towards the city centre to Folly Bridge, then turn right along the Thames towpath on the south side of the river.)

Beyond the farm, keep straight on to the river. Turn right along the towpath. After quarter of a mile or so, the towpath crosses two footbridges over the Weirs Mill Stream (Longbridges Nature Park lies between the two streams). Just beyond this point is a weather-beaten and vandalised stone by the towpath marking the boundary of the City of Oxford. Pass under Donnington Bridge, and keep on along the river back to the Isis. Return to Iffley village the way you came. If you want to see a little more of Iffley village, turn left at the top of the path from the lock, then at the end of Mill lane, turn right along Church Way.

Walk 14

KEY

- - - - - FOOTPATH
═ ═ ═ ═ ═ TRACK
════════ METALLED ROAD
≣≣≣≣≣≣ MAJOR ROAD
▬▬▬▬▬ RAILWAY LINE
〰〰〰 RIVER
✝ CHURCH
□ BUILDING
→ ROUTE OF WALK
⌀ PUBLIC HOUSE

✳ START POINT OF WALK

▱ LAKE OR POND

PUB DETAILS

THE START POINT PUBLIC
HOUSE IS THE ISIS TAVERN
AT IFFLEY.
OTHER PUB FEATURED:-
THE GENERAL ELIOTT
AT SOUTH HINKSEY.

NOTE

THIS MAP IS DIAGRAMMATIC
ONLY AND IS NOT TO SCALE.

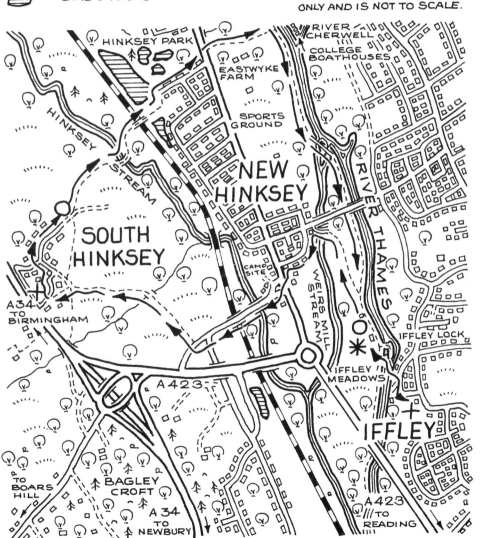
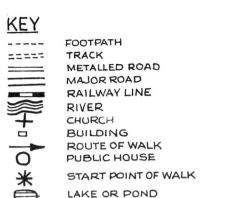

Along the Cherwell and through the Parks from Marston

Maps
Landranger 1:50,000
Sheet 164
Pathfinder 1:25,000
Sheet 1116 (SP 40/50)
Map Reference of Start/
Finish SP520090

How to get there
The Victoria Arms lies
alongside the River Cherwell
at the end of a lane from
Marston village. Marston can
be reached from the A40
Northern Bypass at a minor
interchange north of the Green
Road roundabout in
Headington (follow signs to
Old Marston) or from
Marston Ferry Road between
Summertown and
Headington. Whichever way
you come, follow the main
road though the village, then
turn off into Mill Lane (a no-
through road). Pass the 17th-
century manor house on an S-
bend, then turn left into the
driveway to the Victoria
Arms. Although Marston
village is served by a number
of bus services (including
Oxford Bus Company route
72), walkers relying on public
transport will find it easier to
join the route midway round
near Magdalen Bridge at the
bottom of the High in Oxford.

Background to the Walk

For much of this walk you may be entertained by the antics of punters steering their craft inexpertly up and down the Cherwell. Punts can be hired by the hour from Cherwell Boathouse (off Banbury Road) or Magdalen Bridge, but beware — experts make it look easy — overhanging trees and pole-grabbing mud can prove menacing to the inexperienced.

During a 19th-century outing to 'ride the franchises' (a boundary-checking exercise), the Mayor and Corporation visited a number of public houses. While crossing the ferry at Marston, their long heavy robes hampered them to such an extent that the boat capsized. A small piece of the golden mayoral mace was never recovered, and presumably still lies buried in the mud at the bottom of the Cherwell.

Apart from providing much amusement, the punts contribute to the quintessential Oxford scene of the willow-lined river and the University Parks with its picnickers and cricketers. The Parks, through which this walk passes, is the only place in England where visitors can watch first-class cricket, including matches against the major counties and touring test teams, for free (although a collection is taken and seats must be paid for).

At its southern end, this walk goes close to the centre of Oxford, but takes in parts of the city that are seldom found on the average tourist itinerary. The old manor house at Holywell and the adjacent Church of St. Cross are a case in point. The manor house (part of Balliol College since 1930) was originally built in the early 16th century. The key to St. Cross can be had from the

Pub facilities
Victoria Arms, Marston
(Pictured left)
The Victoria Arms (known affectionately as the Vicky Arms) is popular with punters, being within half-an-hour's punting distance of the Cherwell Boathouse. It is leased by Wadworth's from the Oxford Preservation Trust. It has a large grassy garden with a superior climbing frame for children. The building is first mentioned as a fisherman's cottage in the 1871 census, but the old part of the pub (which includes a semi-circular roofed bread oven) is older than this. The original pub was called The Ferry, as the Marston Ferry crossed the Cherwell here and was operated by the pub staff. There are plans to build a footbridge on the site of the old ferry. The landlord tells me that the garden flooded in the winter of 1992/93 and punters were able to step from their boats onto the grassy bank behind the climbing frame. The daytime menu includes the usual sandwiches, filled jacket potatoes and pub standards plus changing daily specials (such as beef, Guinness and orange pie or celery, stilton and walnut ragout). Several vegetarian choices are always available, as are children's meals. Typical dishes on the evening menu might include red snapper, game pie or seafood kebabs in a creole sauce. There is a good range of real ales on sale; regulars including Wadworth's 6X, Farmer's Glory, Tanglefoot and Henry's Old IPA are supplemented by a guest beer which changes

Porter's Lodge here. The church has a Norman chancel arch (c. 1160) and tower.

Next to the church is Holywell Cemetery, the final resting place of many famous sons of the city, notably Kenneth Grahame (author of *Wind in the Willows*) and Sir John Stainer, the composer. More recently, Kenneth Tynan, playwright, critic and manager of the National Theatre, was buried here in 1980. This cemetery, like Highgate in London, was created in the 19th century to house ex-members of the expanding population, who were otherwise threatening to overwhelm the small burial grounds of the city churches. Nowadays it is maintained as a nature reserve by BBONT and has a peaceful atmosphere of faded Victorian grandeur among the birdsong and wild flowers.

A short distance from the cemetery is Longwall Garage, where William Morris (later Lord Nuffield) built the prototype of the first 'bullnose' Morris Oxford in 1912. The crenellated wall opposite the garage, often taken to be the medieval city wall, is relatively modern. The genuine article surrounds the gardens of New College and can be glimpsed between the buildings on the *right-hand* side of Longwall Street.

Our route leads past several Oxford colleges, including Wolfson and Lady Margaret Hall in the opening stages on the banks of the Cherwell. The only 'old' college *en route* is Magdalen, founded in 1458, whose famous bell tower (completed in 1509) overlooks the *every fortnight. Guinness, various lagers and ciders are also served on draught. The wine list is fairly long, and three of these wines (two white and one red) are available by the glass. Fruit wines by the glass are a speciality. The Victoria Arms is open all day in summer and from 1130-1400 and 1800-2300 in winter. Food is served 1200-1400 and 1900-2100 (except Sunday nights). Children and dogs are welcome. Tel. 0865 241382.*

*There are four other pubs in Marston village (the pretty **Bricklayers Arms** behind the church, the **White Hart** and **Three Horseshoes** next to each other in Oxford Road, and the **Red Lion** on the opposite side). A few minutes from the route in Bath Place (off Holywell Street), the **Turf Tavern** is a famous but hard-to-find Oxford watering hole. There are also several pubs and eating places (ranging from cheap takeaways to upmarket restaurants) in St. Clement's.*

Longwall Garage, where the 'bullnose' Morris was conceived

Cherwell and the Botanic Gardens at Magdalen Bridge. The Bridge itself dates from 1772 and was recently restored following a public appeal.

Near Magdalen Bridge is a roundabout known as The Plain. A turnpike once stood here, alongside the old St. Clement's church. The old church was replaced in 1828 by the neo-Norman church of St. Clement in Marston Road. This building is a rare example of a short-lived revival of interest in Romanesque architecture, inspired by the church at Iffley (see Walk 14). It contains the oldest bell in Oxford, which was cast in the 13th century and transferred from the old church. The curate of the church at the time of the move was John Henry Newman, who was prominent in the Oxford Movement, converted to Catholicism in 1845, and became Cardinal Newman in 1879.

Another name that crops up during this walk is that of Baron Florey. Florey shared the Nobel Prize for Medicine in 1945 with E. B. Chain and Alexander Fleming for their work on penicillin. He is remembered by the dedication of the modern Florey Building in St. Clement's, and by a memorial in the porch of Marston church.

The old village of St. Clement's was largely destroyed during the Civil War, not in open conflict but due to the building of defences and demolition to prevent invaders hiding in the buildings. The Black Horse was one of the few buildings to survive. The inhabitants of St. Clement's suffered again during the cholera epidemic of 1832, especially those living in the streets running down to the Cherwell. Of 174 cases in Oxford, 74 came from St. Clement's.

Marston village also has an interesting history: the church was first mentioned in 1122, when it would have stood on what was virtually an island in a swampy area (hence Marston, 'marsh town'). The village was a Parliamentarian stronghold in the Civil War, and the church tower was used by the Roundheads to spy on Royalist artillery in the Gun Parks (now the University Parks) during the Siege of Oxford. The Roundheads built earthworks in the fields around Marston; contemporary earthworks were also built in the meadow now occupied by Holywell Cemetery. The Treaty of Oxford, by which the Royalists surrendered after Charles I had escaped in disguise from the city, was signed in the Mansion House in 1645.

A more homely event occurred in 1815 when the Reverend John Russell, on a walk to Elsfield, bought a dog called Trump from a milkman in Marston. The dog proved to be 'the perfect fox-terrier' and was the first example of the famous breed named after its master.

The return route takes in the famous waterside walk known as Mesopotamia. A typical Oxford joke this — Mesopotamia coming from the Greek for 'between rivers'. In the Middle East, the rivers are the Tigris and the Euphrates — here they are the Cherwell and an adjacent mill stream.

The walk can be extended by a stroll around Christ Church Meadows, the Botanic Gardens or Magdalen College Deer Park (the first of these is free; a fee is charged for the other two). A detour into central Oxford is also possible, but this is probably better saved for a separate expedition.

Walk 15

Distance: *Even allowing for the minimum of sightseeing, this walk of six miles will take about three-and-a-half hours.*

Note: Most of the walk is along metalled or gravelled paths, including an unavoidable mile or so of urban pavement (in mitigation, there is much of interest on this stretch). Please note that part of the path runs through the University Parks, which are closed in the evenings. Closing times vary according to the season and are displayed at the entrances to the Parks. After heavy rainfall, parts of the path alongside the Cherwell may be subject to flooding.

Take the footpath from the south-eastern corner of the Victoria Arms' garden by the climbing apparatus, and cross a small footbridge. An obvious footpath through some trees leads parallel and close to the River Cherwell. When you reach Marston Ferry Road, cross carefully to regain the footpath on the other side. The John Radcliffe Hospital is prominent on the hillside to the left; just to the right of the white hospital building, the floodlights of Oxford United Football Club are also visible. Keep along the Cherwell to the entrance to Wolfson College Nature Reserve, then take the right-hand fork that continues along the river. The modern buildings of Wolfson College on the far bank of the river reflect the fact that the college is one of the newer Oxford colleges, having been founded in the 1960s. Do not cross the footbridge over the Cherwell that leads to the College. A board by the bridge explains the history, natural value and management of the reserve.

Keeping on along the river, you pass through a gap in a hedge and soon find yourself opposite the Cherwell Boathouse. A stile and footbridge mark the end of the nature reserve — turn left (away from the river briefly) in a small copse, then turn right to cross a footbridge over a side-stream and return to the main riverbank. The imposing buildings of Lady Margaret Hall can be seen beyond the river on the right. Just past the College, you cross a further footbridge over a side-stream; on the other side of the river a large round pond marks the beginning of the University Parks. Keep on along the Cherwell to a high arched footbridge called Rainbow Bridge, where a gravelly path leads off to the left (we shall return this way later). Turn *right* and cross the bridge over the Cherwell into the Parks. Since the route returns along the riverside path on your left, you may like to avoid walking the same ground twice by keeping straight on at the foot of the bridge to see a little more of the Parks — in particular the famous cricket pitch which has been graced by many great players. There are several paths to the left which run parallel to the river. Any of these will lead you to the continuation of our route, a combined foot and cycle path (Mesopotamia Walk) that runs from east to west across the Parks. If in doubt, return to the foot of the bridge and follow the river downstream. When you reach Mesopotamia Walk, which has railings on the north (Parks) side and looks over a hedge to New College Sports Ground to the south, turn right. This leads to the corner of South Parks Road by Linacre College and opposite the Zoology and Psychology Department of the University. Turn left along St. Cross Road, passing the entrance to the Sports Ground, and then the St. Cross Building, on the left. Shortly after this latter building, you reach Holywell Manor at the end of Manor Road, and the squat tower of St. Cross church. The entrance to the Holywell Cemetery is just past the church on the left, next to the old Church School. Once you have visited the Cemetery, keep on along St. Cross Road, which becomes Longwall Street at the junction with the picturesque Holywell Street (to the right). Just here can be seen the Longwall Garage (with a display in the window giving details of the life of William Morris) and glimpses of the city wall between the buildings on the right. Keep on down Longwall Street, with the walls of Magdalen College on the left, until you reach the High. Turn left, passing Magdalen College on the left and the Botanic Gardens on the right, to reach Magdalen Bridge.

Cross the bridge, over the Cherwell and the Angel Meadow on the left, to the Plain. Turn left along St. Clement's. Notice the striking polygonal Florey Building (built 1968-70) behind the car park on the left, and the Stone's Court hospital (1700) on the right. At the bottom of South Park (by the traffic lights) pass a Georgian-style terrace of town houses, then turn left into Marston Road by the Plasterers Arms pub. Pass St. Clement's church on the left, then the Department of Social Security offices on the right. Just before you reach Magdalen College Sports Ground, turn left down a metalled lane. This leads by an old mill and along the famous stretch of path, between two strands of the Cherwell, known as Mesopotamia.

Walk 15

KEY

- - - -	FOOTPATH
=====	TRACK
=====	METALLED ROAD
≈≈≈≈	MAJOR ROAD
	RIVER
+	CHURCH
□	BUILDING
→	ROUTE OF WALK
○	PUBLIC HOUSE
✳	START POINT OF WALK
⬯	LAKE OR POND

PUB DETAILS

THE START POINT PUBLIC HOUSE
IS THE VICTORIA ARMS AT
MARSTON.
OTHER PUBS FEATURED :-
1. THE BRICKLAYERS ARMS
   AT MARSTON.
2. THE TURF TAVERN AT
   BATH PLACE, OXFORD

NOTE

THIS MAP IS DIAGRAMMATIC
ONLY AND IS NOT TO SCALE.

At the end of this stretch, you reach a set of wooden gates; cross the stream to the left, then turn right to reach the weir beyond (bypassed by punts via a set of rollers). Just upstream is Parson's Pleasure, a (recently closed) male nudist bathing area. Turn left and cross another strand of the river. Take the kissing gate on the right into the Parks proper and walk upstream to Rainbow Bridge (by which you crossed the river on the outward leg of the journey). Cross over once again, but this time keep straight on, away from the river. An iron boundary post dated 1886 and bearing the names of the Mayor and Sheriff of Oxford stands by an old ditch. Keep straight on, with distant glimpses of Headington House (home of the late Robert Maxwell) among the trees on the hillside to your right. When you reach a T-junction of paths by St. Catherine's Sports Ground, turn left. This leads to a crossroads of paths by a footbridge; ignore the footbridge and turn right, with the sports field on your right and Marston Brook on the left. This path leads for nearly half a mile along the brook, behind the houses of New Marston, until it emerges in a road by Marston Middle School. Keep straight on until the road swings round to the left by St. Nicholas Primary School, then turn right into a subway decorated with an abstract mural (and the inevitable graffiti). Turn left to pass under Marston Ferry Road, then turn right to reach Oxford Road. Turn left into Marston village and walk past a number of attractive cottages, farmhouses and pubs.

When you reach Mill Lane on the left, you can return directly to the Victoria Arms, but a recommended diversion around the village is as follows. Turn right into Elsfield Road (signposted to St. Nicholas Church). When you reach the church, walk through the churchyard to the back gate by the Bricklayers Arms. Turn left along Ponds Lane to emerge by the Manor House, then turn right. The entrance to the Victoria Arms is on the left.

Port Meadow, Oxford's finest green space

WALK 16
Allow 3 hours
6 miles
Walk begins page 98

Background to the Walk

Within seconds of leaving the bustle of Hythe Bridge Street, you will find yourself walking a quiet stretch of the Oxford Canal towpath and, apart from a minor interlude in Wolvercote village, the scenery is rural from then on. The canal was built in 1790 and originally terminated at a wharf south of Hythe Bridge Street, on what is now the site of Worcester Street car park.

The main attraction of this walk is the 345 acres of common land at Port Meadow. Geese, horses and cattle may be grazed on the Meadow by Freemen and Commoners of the city. It is said that a distinguished American visitor once asked to see the oldest monument in the city; the locals who led him to Port Meadow had some justification, for the grazing arrangements, substantially the same as they are today, were noted in the Domesday survey of 1087. To prevent unauthorized grazing, the animals on the Meadow are rounded up once a year and impounded in a compound near Wolvercote. Legitimate owners can retrieve their animals for a small fee; owners of unauthorized stock are fined. The pound was once at Gloucester Green, now the city's main coach station. The round-up is conducted by the Sheriff of Oxford, whose predecessors have left their mark on the Meadow — Sheriff's Bridge is named after Sheriff Hunt who built it in 1841, and a series of metal boundary posts bear the name of Sheriff Twining who held the office in 1886.

Port Meadow is unusual in that it has never been ploughed or sprayed with pesticides; this makes it an important area for wildlife. When the Meadow was in danger of becoming overgrown by the invasive weed

Maps
Landranger 1:50,000
Sheet 164
Pathfinder 1:25,000
Sheet 1116 (SP 40/50)
Map Reference of Start/
Finish SP508063

How to get there
Antiquity Hall is in Hythe Bridge Street, close to Oxford city centre. Car-drivers are recommended to use the cheap Park-and-Ride bus services from the outskirts of the city (where there are large free car parks) or the pay-and-display Worcester Street car park in the centre. Train and bus travellers can choose from a large number of services to the city; Oxford rail station is close to the starting point, as is the coach station at Gloucester Green.

Pub facilities
Antiquity Hall, Oxford
Recently revamped, this large pub in Hythe Bridge Street belies its quaint name, having a young clientele and a lively atmosphere. Nonetheless it has a long history, recounted on a framed poster on the wall. In the 18th century it served the bargemen and fishermen of the surrounding area. It was also a favourite watering hole of the antiquarian Thomas Hearne and his cronies, who

probably inspired its original name. It was later known as The Nag's Head, then Navigation House, and then The Nag's Head again, until the original name was restored in 1992. The address is strictly 1-2 Fisher Island; the pub lies on an island in the Castle Mill Stream, a Thames tributary. A riverside terrace overlooks part of the stream, where there are usually ducks to be fed. Food for humans (lunchtimes only) includes snacks (filled baguettes, soup, garlic bread, Mexican salad, etc.) and main meals such as steak and kidney pie or chicken Kiev. As well as the regular Tetley's and Burton ales, there is a fortnightly guest beer, plus the usual range of lagers, ciders and Guinness. Children are welcome at lunchtime and in the early evenings, as are dogs on leads. There is no car parking available at the pub, but Worcester Street car park is only just around the corner. Opening hours are currently 1100-1430 and 1730-2300 (except Sundays, when the usual Sunday hours apply), but there are plans to introduce all-day opening. Tel. 0865 249153.

*Two famous riverside pubs, the **Perch** at Binsey and the **Trout Inn** at Godstow, are passed en route. There are two less well-known pubs in Wolvercote village, the **Red Lion** and the **White Hart**.*

Antiquity Hall, Oxford

Oxford Ragwort (which spread throughout the country along railway lines from a few original specimens in the Botanic Garden in Oxford), volunteers stepped in to uproot the plants by hand. The Meadow is important in maintaining the River Thames at safe levels; floodwater can safely accumulate here rather than inundating built-up areas downstream. This importance is recognised by Thames Water and the City Council, who discourage development on the flood plain. Occasionally the floodwaters freeze, and in the past large numbers of people took to the ice on skates; old photographs of such events show an evocative scene reminiscent of a Breughel painting. Nowadays, skaters are more likely to use the new indoor skating rink a little further downstream!

When flooded, the Meadow attracts large flocks of Lapwings, Golden Plover, Canada Geese and Black-headed Gulls, which are sometimes joined by waders (such as Ruff and Redshank) and ducks (such as Wigeon, Shoveler, Teal and Pintail). Domestic geese grazing on the Meadow have sometimes hybridized with wild geese to produce a strain known as the Port Meadow Special. An unusual ornithological occurrence was witnessed at Godstow Lock — two Kingfishers collided in mid-air, and the two birds, impaled on each other's beaks, fell to the ground stone dead. The book in which this story is recounted, *The Oxford Country* by R. T. Günther, includes a drawing of the interlocked skulls of the birds in question.

In the past Port Meadow has been used for horse racing, and as a World War I airfield. An early flying disaster claimed the lives of two officers of the Royal Flying Corps when their monoplane crashed near Wolvercote in 1912. They are commemorated by a plaque in the wall at Wolvercote Bridge.

A raised area on the eastern side of the Meadow was a rubbish tip until 1982. In 1978, Colin Dexter wrote of the tip in *Last Seen Wearing*: 'Doubtless grass and shrubs would soon be burgeoning there, and the animals would return to their old territories and scurry once more in the hedgerows amid the bracken and the wild flowers.' His words were prophetic — this eyesore has become an amenity, the Burgess Field Nature Park, which shows what a little investment and imagination can achieve. Already, local rarities such as wintering Stonechat and Short-eared Owl have been seen here.

At the northern end of the Meadow is Godstow Abbey or Nunnery. The existing remains mainly date from the 15th and 16th centuries, but the abbey was founded in around 1133. Its consecration was attended by King Stephen and his courtiers. Walter de Clifford sent his daughter Rosamund here to be educated. Henry II took her as his mistress and installed her in a house near his home at Woodstock Manor (see Walk 19). She was supposedly poisoned by Henry's jealous wife, Eleanor of Aquitaine, but the truth is probably that she returned to Godstow and died of natural causes. The abbey building was later converted into a mansion, Godstow House, but it was severely damaged in the Civil War and abandoned. Subsequently it was used as a source of building stone by Wolvercote villagers (the remains of a 15th-century doorway in the wall above a window of the Red Lion in Wolvercote may have come from here). In the 19th and early 20th century the ruin was used as a pound for livestock rounded up from the Meadow; the walls may have been partially rebuilt, and a well dug in the centre, for this purpose. The most complete part nowadays is the chapel in the corner nearest to Godstow Lock.

There was a bridge over the Thames at Godstow at the time the Abbey was built, but the three existing bridges are 18th century. Charles Dodgson (Lewis Carroll) is said to have first told his stories of Alice on boat trips from Oxford to Godstow. Between the bridges is the Trout Inn, which was once the guest-house of the Abbey. It is thought to have been an inn since at least 1625. The wooden bridge to the island has been in a ramshackle condition for some years and now does not even reach the far bank. On the island (not accessible to the public) is a garden with several statues, which were installed early this century. Fish sometimes break the surface of the weir pool to engulf small pieces of bread or crisps thrown from the terrace — however, these are usually chub rather than trout. This famous pub has featured more than once in *Inspector Morse*; in one TV episode the author, Colin Dexter, made one of his famous cameo appearances reading a newspaper at a table behind Morse and Lewis. The pub also featured recently in the BBC1 police series *Between The Lines*. The last stage of the walk follows the Oxford Canal, passing the suburb of Jericho on the opposite bank. Thomas Hardy used the neighbourhood as the model for Beersheba in *Jude The Obscure*. The Byzantine church of St.

Barnabas, with its unusual campanile and vast mosaic-covered interior, appears in the novel as 'the ceremonial church of St. Silas'.

Walk 16

Distance: *Allow about three hours for this six mile walk which includes canal and river towpaths, and a stroll across part of Port Meadow.*
Note: Although most of the paths are slightly above the lowest parts of the Meadow, floods occur every winter and some of the route may be impassable at such times.

Cross Hythe Bridge Street and turn right over the bridge. Turn left immediately beyond the bridge, alongside the Castle Mill Stream. After a few yards you reach the end of the Oxford Canal on your right. Keep along between the canal and the Castle Mill Stream. A hundred yards or so from Hythe Bridge Street, look carefully between the trees at the wall beyond the stream on the left for a simple archway; this is the former water gate (and sole surviving remnant) of Rewley Abbey. When you reach Isis Lock (one of two connections between the Oxford Canal and the Thames), cross the smartly painted metal bridge (of 1796), then cross the Castle Mill Stream by a further footbridge. The path leads around an abandoned swing-bridge, across which railway wagons were once shunted to sidings to the north, then passes below the main railway line under a low bridge.

When you reach the main navigation channel of the Thames turn right, away from the footbridge on your left. This path leads attractively between the Thames and the Fiddler's Island Stream on the right. After about half a mile you reach Medley Boat Station. Keep alongside the main river for as long as possible, with the boat basin on the right, then cross a footbridge to the western bank. Turn right and follow the towpath past the boat yard. After a further half-mile of riverside walking, with extensive views of the Meadow on the opposite side of the river, pass the end of a track to Binsey village on the left. Just beyond this point, before a grey-painted NRA gate, a path leads over a stile to the Perch, a thatched pub with a large garden. Continue along the towpath for about a mile, until you reach Godstow Lock. Keep on past the lock to Godstow Bridge, passing the ruins of Godstow Abbey on the left. When you reach the road, turn right and cross two narrow bridges to the entrance to the Trout Inn. Continue over a third bridge and pass Port Meadow Picnic Area, which has a car park and public conveniences.

Walk on through Wolvercote, passing the White Hart and the Red Lion, a fish and chip shop and the Post Office. When you reach a small metal gate on the right (erected to commemorate the Queen's Silver Jubilee in 1977) pass through onto a cinder track that leads across Wolvercote Common to the railway. Walk parallel to the railway, then away from it around a ditched and hedged field. Just beyond the apex of this field is a wide and low stone bridge over a ditch. Cross this bridge, then keep left past a metal boundary marker, bearing the name of Sheriff Twining. A little way on, cross a footbridge and a stile that leads up the bank to a second stile and so into Burgess Field Nature Park. Turn right around the edge of the Nature

Walk 16

KEY

- - - -	FOOTPATH
====	TRACK
	METALLED ROAD
	MAJOR ROAD
	RAILWAY LINE
+++	RAILWAY SIDING
～～	RIVER
	CANAL
+	CHURCH
▭	BUILDING
➡	ROUTE OF WALK
○	PUBLIC HOUSE
✳	START POINT OF WALK
∥∥∥	HILL FEATURE

PUB DETAILS

THE START POINT PUBLIC HOUSE IS THE ANTIQUITY HALL IN OXFORD.

OTHER PUBS FEATURED :—
1). THE PERCH (BINSEY)
2). THE TROUT (GODSTOW)
3). WHITE HART (Lʷᴿ WOLVERCOTE)
4). RED LION (Lʷᴿ WOLVERCOTE)

NOTE

THIS MAP IS DIAGRAMMATIC ONLY AND IS NOT TO SCALE.

Park, with good views over the Meadow. In season, blackberry bushes here are laden with fruit.

Part way along, a short distance out into the Meadow on the right is an insignificant hump in the ground. This is the Round Hill, believed to be a Bronze Age burial mound. It is recorded that some literal-minded Victorians had the mound reshaped so

Isis Lock, the first lock on the Oxford Canal

that it might live up to its name. Straight ahead there are views to the Radcliffe Observatory and the Radcliffe Camera. When you meet a gravelly track, keep right. This leads to the corner of the Nature Park, where a stile and footbridge and a stock-proof metal bridge lead out onto Port Meadow. Cross the bridge, then keep left along a raised concrete track. When this divides, ignore the turning to the left that leads up to Aristotle Bridge, and keep straight on along the track. This leads to a car park approximately level with Medley Boat Station on the far side of the Meadow. Pass the gate into the car park, then walk left up the road and over the railway. Just beyond, two stone eagles guard the entrance to a workshop on the left; take a path on the right which leads down a ramp and under a bridge to the Oxford Canal. Turn right. The canal shows its industrial origins as it passes in front of a large factory. The towpath passes under a footbridge to some flats on the left-hand bank (this gives access to Jericho), then past a couple of boatyards near St. Barnabas church. Beyond the boatyards the towpath skirts a small turning basin just before Isis Lock. Cross the iron bridge once more and retrace your steps to Hythe Bridge Street and Antiquity Hall.

Along the Oxfordshire Way on the edge of Otmoor

Background to the Walk

Otmoor has a special atmosphere, and seems out of place in pastoral Oxfordshire. John Buchan (who set his novel *The Blanket of the Dark* here) said of Otmoor 'to ride or walk there in an Autumn twilight is to find oneself in a place as remote from man as Barra or Knoydart.' To compare Otmoor with the emptinesses of the Scottish Highlands is perhaps a bit strong, but compared to the surrounding countryside, the moor is still something of a wilderness. It was a huge marshy wasteland until it was drained and enclosed in the early 19th century. One of the exponents of agricultural improvement was Arthur Young, the Secretary to the Board of Agriculture. He considered that it was a 'scandal to the national policy' that such a large area should support only small numbers of livestock at a time when agricultural imports were high, despite noting that cattle grazed on the damp pastures suffered from 'moor evil', and sheep from foot-rot. He believed that the latter arose from 'stagnant waters, and more peculiarly from the disgustful effluvia arising from their weedy beds in sunny weather'.

There was vigorous opposition to enclosure from locals, who wished to retain their rights to raise geese, graze sheep and harvest reeds for thatching and willows for basket-making. Local farmers vandalised the dykes and fences, and 44 men were arrested and taken to Oxford. The troops foolishly paraded their captives in front of the throng at St. Giles' Fair; the local populace promptly set upon them and the men escaped.

Otmoor has been the cause of protest again in recent times — in the 1970s it was threatened by plans to build

Maps
Landranger 1:50,000
Sheet 164
Pathfinder 1:25,000
Sheet 1092 (SP 41/51)
Map Reference of Start/
Finish SP565113

How to get there
Beckley is north-east of Oxford, just off the B4027 Wheatley to Islip road. From the Green Road roundabout where the A40 meets the Oxford Ring Road, take the unclassified road signposted to Oxford Crematorium. Ignore a right-hand turning to Stanton St. John, then on reaching the B4027 turn left then first right. In Beckley village, keep right by the church to reach the Abingdon Arms. Beckley is served by the very infrequent Yellow Bus service M37 — contact Motts Travel on 0296 613831 for details.

Pub facilities

Abingdon Arms, Beckley
This stone-built pub is over
300 years old, and is
distinguished by its beautiful
terrace and sloping garden,
with a goldfish pond and
fountain, a summer house and
fruit trees. The pub was
owned by the Earls of
Abingdon until the start of the
20th century, and was
frequented by Evelyn Waugh
in the late 1920s. The summer
menu includes salads such as
salmon, smoked chicken, Greek
salad with tarama, and
farmhouse cheddar cheese with
tomato, crudités, chutney and
apple. In the winter, heartier
dishes are on offer, such as
bouillabaisse, chicken curry
with poppadum and chutney,
and baked aubergine with
apricots and lentils. Drinks
include Wadworth's 6X,
Adnam's Bitter, Lowenbrau
lager, Guinness and
Copperhead cider (all on
draught). Over 30 wines are
available by the bottle. The
Abingdon Arms also serves a
range of foreign bottled lagers,
wine by the glass and a
number of malt whiskies.
Children are welcome in the
garden, as are dogs on leads
(also in the public bar, with
permission from the landlord).
If you have fallen foul of
Otmoor's notorious mud,
please use the public bar. If
you wish to leave your car in
the car park while you walk,
check with the landlord before
you set off. Opening hours are
1130-1430 and 1830-2300
during the week, and 1200-
1430 and 2000-2230 on
Sundays. Food is served from
1215-1345 and from 1915-
2115, except on Sunday
evenings.
Tel. 0865 351311.

The Abingdon Arms in Beckley

a reservoir, and in the late '80s it was identified as a possible route for the M40 motorway extension. Fortunately both proposals were abandoned in the face of strong local opposition. Despite extensive drainage, on summer evenings when the mist lies low over the boggy meadows it has a unique atmosphere. It is an SSSI (Site of Special Scientific Interest) and supports an unusual community of wildlife. Wading birds such as Snipe, Curlew and Lapwing breed here, as do Grasshopper Warblers and Nightingales (another reason to undertake this walk on a summer evening). It is also the best place in the county to see and hear owls.

Botanically, it is just as interesting and even boasts its own plant, the 'Otmoor violet' (thought to be a hybrid of the Heath Dog Violet and Fen Violet), as well as a number of rare sedges and other damp-loving plants. Rare insects include the Black Hairstreak and Marsh Fritillary butterflies, and the Emperor Moth. This natural interest comes at a price: the paths are frequently very muddy, although this route avoids the very wettest parts of the moor. Boots or Wellingtons are recommended in all but the driest of dry spells.

Probably the most valuable part of the moor for wildlife is around the Rifle Range, where the effects of drainage have been felt the least. The Rifle Range is still active. However, this route does not enter the Danger Area, so none of the paths are closed during firing (this

Your guides to local events in Beckley

is not true of some of the paths across the centre of the moor). Because of the proximity of the range, access to the BBONT reserve is by permit only — contact BBONT at 2 Church Cowley Road, Rose Hill, Oxford OX4 3JR (tel. 0865 775476).

Our starting point, Beckley (one of the 'seven towns of Otmoor'), is a pretty stone village perched high above the moor. The view of Otmoor may have inspired Lewis Carroll to write in *Through The Looking Glass* — 'They walked on in silence till they got to the top of the hill. For some minutes Alice stood without speaking, looking out in all directions over the country — and a most curious country it was. There were a number of tiny little brooks running straight across it from side to side, and the ground between was divided up into squares by a number of little green hedges, that reached from brook to brook. "I declare it's marked out just like a large chess-board" Alice said at last.'

Beckley has a very interesting church, built to a Norman ground plan with a central tower. The most noticeable feature as you enter the church is the wall painting of the Last Judgement or Doom. To the left of the arch are depicted the souls of the saved entering the gates of heaven; to the right the damned in the jaws of hell. In the south aisle there are more diabolical scenes graphically described in the church guide — 'St. Michael holds a balance in his hands. To the left a figure of the devil tries to pull the scale in his favour. Above, the Torments of the Damned. A body is roasting on a spit, the flames fanned by bellows, the body basted by a devilish creature above. To the left, the next victim awaits its turn, hanging by the feet from a meat-hook.'

There are two fine houses glimpsed during the walk. Beckley Park was originally owned by King Alfred, though the existing moated house was built in the 16th century. Aldous Huxley's account of country-house life, *Crome Yellow*, was based on the house. It is not usually open to the public. Studley Priory was originally a Benedictine priory, and is now an hotel. Much of the 1966 Oscar-winning film *A Man For All Seasons* was filmed there.

The first half-mile and last mile of this walk follow the Oxfordshire Way, a 65-mile walking route from Bourton-on-the-Water in the west to Henley-on-Thames in the south-east.

Walk 17

Distance: *Allow about two hours for this walk of just over four miles.*

(Note: This walk may be very muddy after wet weather. There are several gates and stiles to be negotiated.) From the front door of the Abingdon Arms turn right, up the hill through the village, passing a telephone box on the left. When you reach the church, turn right into Church Street. There are several exceptionally pretty cottages here. Look out to your right for your first views of Otmoor. Beyond the last house, the lane becomes a track and descends more steeply; keep on to a gate looking out over the moor. An Oxfordshire Way sign points straight on, directly towards the tower of Charlton-on-Otmoor church on the far side of the moor. Don't follow it, but cross the stile on the left and walk diagonally down the field to a further stile in a fence, with Noke Wood behind. In the far corner, there is a third stile leading through a thick hedge. The path then leads alongside a rushy field to the edge of Noke Wood, where it turns left into the wood (don't be tempted by traces of a path leading straight on — this is not a public footpath).

You emerge from the wood at the corner of a large field, with the buildings of Lower Farm visible on the far side. The church towers of Oddington (straight ahead) and Charlton-on-Otmoor (to the right) are both visible from this point. Scan the field for hares (very common hereabouts), then turn right and follow the edge of the wood on your right. At the end of the wood, the path leads on through farmland with a ditch and hedge to the right. Fifty yards on, it swings right over a footbridge. At another footbridge, you meet up once again with the Oxfordshire Way; turn left here. The farm on a slight rise to your right is, confusingly, also called Lower Farm (this is Lower Farm, Beckley; the other farm you saw across the field a few minutes ago was Lower Farm, Noke). A few yards on, the path rises slightly and turns sharply right. There follows a long straight stretch of about half a mile which leads to a gate into Otmoor Lane by the first of many Ministry of Defence warning signs. Just before the gate, turn right then left to cross a footbridge into the lane. The warning signs apply only to the paths across the centre of the moor (to your left); our route turns *right* along Otmoor Lane. This follows the line of a Roman road which led from the garrison at Alcester (near Bicester) to Dorchester and beyond. Shortly you reach a bank of earth and rubble (built to prevent vehicles driving onto Otmoor) by the entrance to the BBONT reserve.

After negotiating the earth bank, take a path on the left through a gap in the hedge by the reserve entrance. This path leads over a stile into a scrubby field (which can get rather muddy). Walk straight ahead along the edge of the field with a thick hedge on the right. In summer, listen for the whirring song of Grasshopper Warblers in this area and look out for the yellow flowers of Dyer's Greenweed, which looks rather like a miniature version of Broom. About 75 yards short of the brick stop butt (a relic of a World War II range that pointed in the opposite direction to the modern one), cross to the other side of the hedge through a stile on the right. Turn left and keep on in the same direction as before, with the hedge

KEY

- - - - - FOOTPATH
═════ TRACK
═════ METALLED ROAD
〰〰 STREAM
✝ CHURCH
▫ BUILDING
➤ ROUTE OF WALK
○ PUBLIC HOUSE
✳ START POINT OF WALK
▏▏▏▏ HILL FEATURE

Walk 17

NOTE

THIS MAP IS
DIAGRAMMATIC ONLY
AND IS NOT TO SCALE

PUB DETAILS

THE START POINT
PUBLIC HOUSE IS THE
ABINGDON ARMS AT
BECKLEY

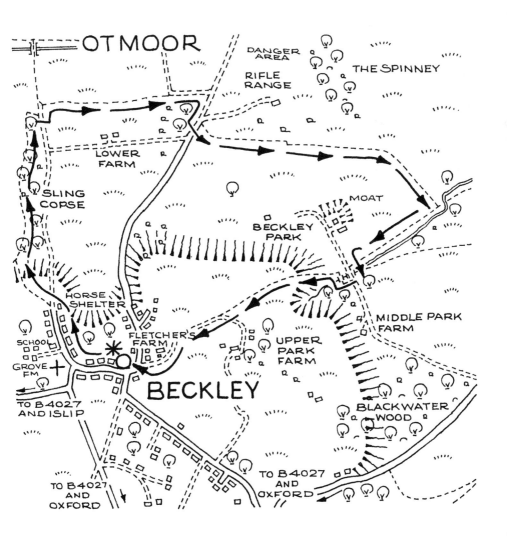

Stone cottages in Church Street, Beckley

now on your left. The chimneys of Beckley Park stand out among the trees on your right and Studley Priory is visible on the hillside in front of you. At the end of this field, you reach a farm gate — cross it and carry straight on. At the far end, pass through a sheep enclosure into a roughly rectangular field. Keep to the left-hand edge. In the corner, a path leads off to the left towards Horton-cum-Studley. Turn *right*, still keeping to the field edge. Ignore a gate on the left to reach a double stile, which leads into a triangular field. At the far end of this field is a kissing gate onto the metalled lane to Beckley Park.

Turn left, then right after a few yards. This pretty path crosses a stile and a footbridge, then follows the stream for a short way. The wooded area on the left marks the site of an ancient fishpond. At the end of the wood, negotiate a stile then walk straight up the hill. There are extensive views of Otmoor and the Rifle Range to the right, and the hilltop village of Brill behind you. At the top of the hill by Upper Park Farm there is a further stile, then the path cuts half-left across the corner of a field to a grassy track by an Oxfordshire Way waymark. Follow this track to the right, with the Beckley TV mast prominent on your left. A little way farther on, you cross the line of the former park pale or boundary (largely invisible on the ground) to reach the outskirts of Beckley at Fletchers Farm. The track leads down steeply through trees to the village. Keep straight on, past a small pond on the left, to return to the Abingdon Arms.

Hampton Gay,
the Oxford Canal
and River Cherwell

WALK 18
Allow 2 hours
4 ¹/₂ miles
Walk begins page 109

Background to the Walk

Regular train travellers from Oxford to Banbury will have noticed that the railway crosses and re-crosses the canal and river many times between the two towns. They may even have glimpsed momentarily two tiny churches, one each side of the railway, as the train thunders between Shipton-on-Cherwell and Hampton Gay. They will certainly not be comforted to learn that this was the scene of a terrible rail accident, which at the time was the worst in the history of railway travel.

The walk begins in Thrupp on the Oxford Canal. The canal was built through the parish in 1788 and opened in 1790, and still benefits the village — boaters and anglers bring trade to the pub (aptly named The Boat Inn), and a number of narrowboats are kept here over winter. British Waterways has a maintenance yard at Thrupp Wide, where you will usually find one or two dredging barges moored. Opposite The Boat Inn is a late medieval cross. The building next to it was used for many years as a chapel. It was opened by the Baptists in 1876 as part of a mission to the canal people. Services were held until 1953 but it has now reverted to its original residential use.

All in all, the combination of brightly painted canal barges, rose-covered canal cottages and the lifting bridge make this a delightful place. Part of Colin Dexter's book *The Riddle of the Third Mile* is set here. The case revolves around a dismembered and hence unidentifiable body found in the canal — Morse and Lewis spend much time pondering the mystery at The Boat Inn.

A short mile north, along the canal, is Shipton-on-Cherwell. This village has a different, leafier feel — the

Maps
Landranger 1:50,000
Sheet 164
Pathfinder 1:25,000
Sheet 1092 (SP 41/51)
Map Reference of Start/
Finish SP481158

How to get there
The walk begins at the Boat Inn at Thrupp. From the A4260 (Banbury Road) just north of Kidlington, take the no-through road signposted to Thrupp. The pub is a couple of hundred yards from the main road, on the left. You could equally well begin at the Gone Fish Inn in Hampton Poyle, signposted from the Kidlington to Bicester road. Hampton Poyle is served from Oxford and Bicester by the following buses: Midland Red service 35, and Thames Transit services 25 and 25A.

Pub facilities
Boat Inn, Thrupp
This old stone-built pub, within sight of the Oxford Canal at Thrupp, was formerly known as the Axe, then the Unicorn. It has been the Boat Inn since about 1839. It is a Morrell's house serving, amongst other things, Morrell's Varsity and Best bitters, Guinness and Stowford Press cider. The spacious main bar has a

display of paintings by a local amateur art group, most of which are for sale. There are two gardens, one in front and one behind the pub. From the front garden you can sit and watch the canal barges going by. Food is simple but well prepared, with French bread 'Crusties', ploughman's lunches, salads, grills and a vegetarian selection on the standard menu. The daily special might be tuna and pasta bake, chilli con carne or curried chicken, for example. Well-behaved children are welcome in the bars and the garden, but dogs may only be brought into the garden, not inside the pub building. Opening hours are 1100-1500 and 1800-2300 on weekdays and Saturdays, and 1200-1500 and 1900-2230 on Sundays. Lunch is served from 1200-1415 seven days a week, and from 1815-2115 in the evenings (1900-2100 on Sunday nights). If you wish to leave your car in the car park while you walk, please ask the landlady before departing. Tel. 0865 374279.

The Boat Inn at Thrupp

church sits in a commanding position overlooking the canal bridge, and is approached by a line of pollarded lime trees. The Manor House, just up the hill from the church, houses Virgin Records' recording studio, where *Tubular Bells* was recorded in 1972-3.

A short distance away, across the canal, river and railway, is Hampton Gay. This village has had a traumatic history. It was once much larger, as the humps and hollows in the surrounding fields testify. Now there is just an 18th-century church standing alone in a field, a ruined 16th-century manor house, a farm and a row of cottages. In 1792, at the height of 'canal mania', there were ambitious plans to build a canal from the Oxford Canal here to London. This canal, to be called the Hampton Gay Canal, or the London and Western, would have bypassed the then difficult journey down the Thames. The plan never came to fruition, and the Grand Junction Canal (which meets the Oxford Canal at Braunston in Northamptonshire) opened in 1805 to exploit the market for an easy cargo route from the Midlands to London.

On Christmas Eve, 1874, the London to Wolverhampton train stopped at Oxford, where an extra carriage was added to the busy train. The train had not travelled far when a metal tyre on the newly added carriage broke. A fault in the alarm system prevented the driver from being made aware of the problem, and by the time he noticed the alarm bell rope moving (but crucially not ringing the bell itself) the rear part of the train had become detached. It ploughed off the rails, down the embankment and into fields alongside the canal, some carriages actually ending up in the water. Twenty-six passengers died immediately, the dead and injured being carried to the paper mill on the Cherwell and to the Elizabethan

**Gone Fish Inn,
Hampton Poyle**
This 17th-century former coaching inn is a Free House that has recently changed hands and, as a consequence, names as well. Until quite recently it was the Bell Inn and appears as such on the map that accompanies this walk. There is an optional diversion on the walk to visit the pub.

Thatched cottages at Thrupp

manor house of Hampton Gay. Here they were attended by a local doctor who had been visiting a patient nearby, and a young doctor who had been a passenger on the doomed train. The injured were eventually taken by train to the Radcliffe Infirmary in Oxford, and others were distributed to various hotels. The final death toll was over thirty. At the GWR inquest the disaster was put down to pure accident, but several safety improvements were recommended by Lord Randolph Churchill, who had gone to the crash scene from Blenheim to help the rescue efforts as soon as he heard of the accident.

Hampton Gay was not spared further disaster. In 1877 there was a fire at the paper mill. Ten years later the mill closed, and in the same year there was a terrible fire at the manor house, leaving it in the ruinous state that you see today.

Hampton Gay's sister village, Hampton Poyle, has an old church with an open belfry. The church is usually locked, but the key can be had at Church Farm, a few yards up the lane on the left. Inside the church is a famous brass of a knight in armour and his lady, dated 1424. The village also boasts a number of fine old stone houses, including Poyle Court, an early 17th-century house with a castellated façade of about 1800. In 1596 an agrarian revolt, organised in Hampton Poyle and supported by workers from Hampton Gay, prompted the Tillage Acts of 1597.

From Hampton Poyle the spire of Kidlington church is clearly visible. Kidlington is one of the largest villages in the country, but the area around the church (worth a detour) retains a rural aspect. The walk returns alongside the River Cherwell (pronounced 'Charwell') to Thrupp.

Walk 18
Distance: Allow two hours for this river and canal-side walk of four-and-a-half miles.
From the garden of the Boat Inn, turn left to reach the canal. Walk along the towpath to the left, between the canal and a row of stone cottages. When you reach the British Waterways Maintenance Depot, cross the lifting bridge and follow the

towpath to the left with the canal on your left. A short distance from the bridge you cross a small weir where overflow from the canal runs into the Cherwell. After a quarter of a mile of towpath walking, you reach the canal bridge at Shipton-on-Cherwell. Our route turns right, away from the canal, but you may like to take a short detour over the canal bridge to look round Shipton village. From the canal bridge, take the path towards Hampton Gay, which leads across a meadow to a footbridge over the River Cherwell, then across another field to the railway.

Cross the railway carefully to emerge in a further field, with Hampton Gay church on the left. A board in the churchyard has more information about the church and village. The path leads straight across to the edge of a clump of trees in front of the ruined Manor House. From here the path leads to a gate under a holly tree, by the Manor Farmhouse. Cross a stile next to the gate into the lane and walk between the few surviving buildings of Hampton Gay. Follow the lane around a bend to the right (ignoring a footpath that leads off to the left up the hill towards Bletchingdon). The lane then passes a small oak copse on the right (Madam Hindes's Spinney); when the lane bends slightly left level with the end of the copse, take a field path on the right (sometimes under crops). This leads to a hedge by the end of the copse, then turns left. This path leads along the left-hand edge of two fields (divided by a footbridge and double stile), then across a couple of fields towards the church at Hampton Poyle. As you approach the church, take a diagonal path across a horse paddock (crossing the wooden fence that divides it) to a stile near the far left-hand corner. This leads round the right-hand edge of a field then over two stiles to Church Lane, Hampton Poyle. From here, walk left along the lane until you reach a crenallated house (Poyle Court) on the left. If you wish to visit the Gone Fish Inn, carry on to the main village street (Oxford Road). The pub is a few yards from the junction of Church Lane and Oxford Road (and is marked on our map as the Bell Inn — it changed its name shortly before this book went to print, but too late for the map to be updated). Return the way you came.

Take the drive opposite Poyle Court. After a few yards, the drive swings left into a house. Follow the path leading straight on, which leads to a stile and then around the right-hand edge of a field to a further stile. Straight ahead across a field you reach a concrete footbridge over the River Cherwell, with the spire of Kidlington church straight ahead. Do not take the path towards the church; instead turn right along the river. Manor Farm and Hampton Poyle church make a fine picture on the right, on the far side of the river. This waymarked path leads through fields alongside the river to a good picnic spot at a notable meander. From this point the public right of way heads away from the river to the left-hand corner of the field, then crosses a small footbridge and heads back towards the river (past a World War II pill box) to reach a bridge under the railway. (A track running alongside the river from the meander to the railway bridge is not a formal right of way, although it appears to be more frequently used than the official route.) Under the railway bridge, you emerge into the maintenance yard at Thrupp. Cross the lifting bridge and turn left to return to the Boat Inn.

KEY

Walk 18

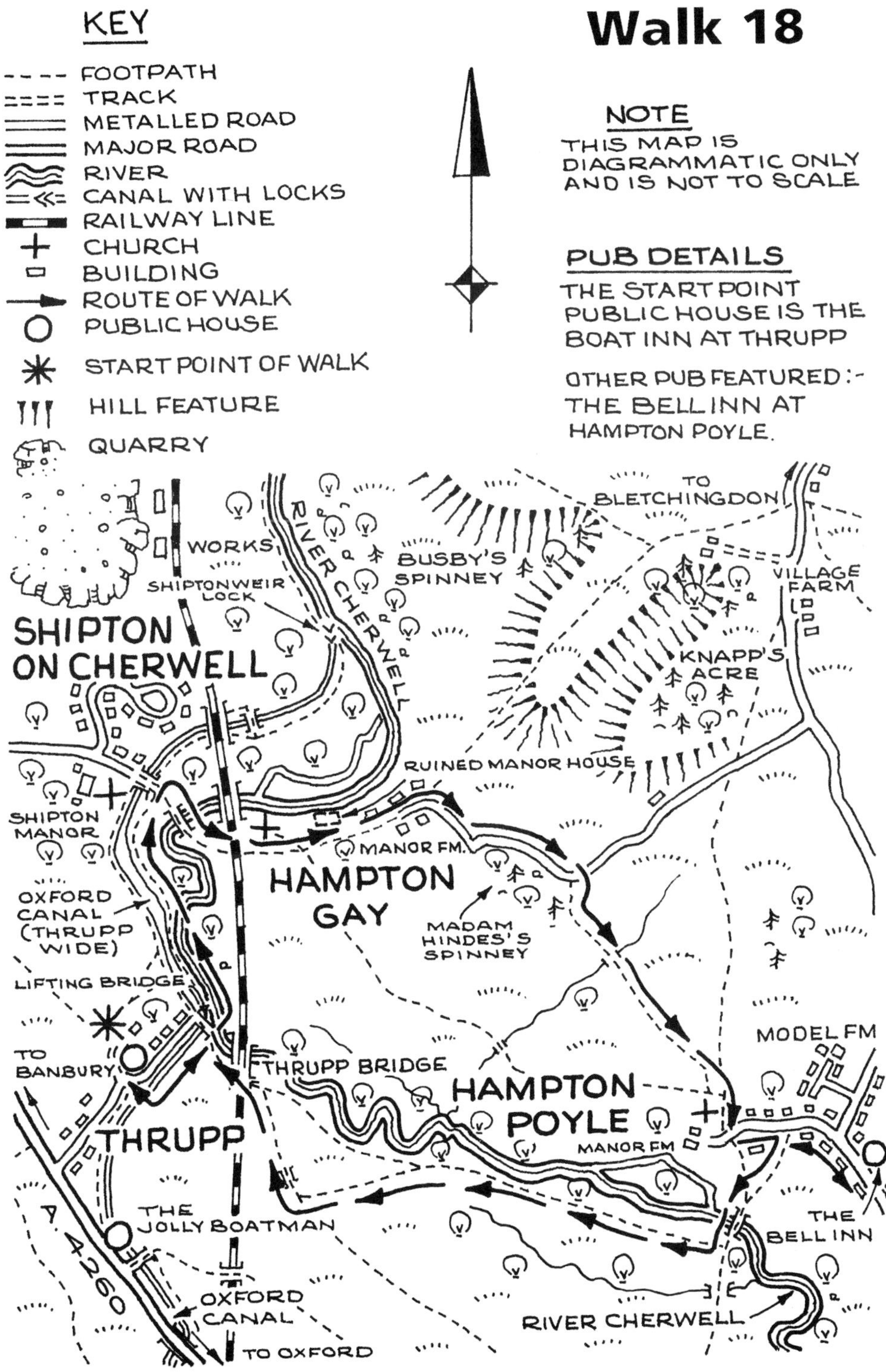

- `- - - -` FOOTPATH
- `= = = =` TRACK
- `———` METALLED ROAD
- `═══` MAJOR ROAD
- `≈≈≈` RIVER
- `=≪=` CANAL WITH LOCKS
- `▪▬▪` RAILWAY LINE
- `+` CHURCH
- `▫` BUILDING
- `——→` ROUTE OF WALK
- `O` PUBLIC HOUSE
- `✳` START POINT OF WALK
- `ᴜᴜᴜ` HILL FEATURE
- QUARRY

NOTE

THIS MAP IS DIAGRAMMATIC ONLY AND IS NOT TO SCALE

PUB DETAILS

THE START POINT PUBLIC HOUSE IS THE BOAT INN AT THRUPP

OTHER PUB FEATURED :-
THE BELL INN AT HAMPTON POYLE.

TO BLETCHINGDON

WORKS

SHIPTONWEIR LOCK

BUSBY'S SPINNEY

VILLAGE FARM

RIVER CHERWELL

SHIPTON ON CHERWELL

KNAPP'S ACRE

RUINED MANOR HOUSE

SHIPTON MANOR

MANOR FM.

HAMPTON GAY

MADAM HINDES'S SPINNEY

OXFORD CANAL (THRUPP WIDE)

LIFTING BRIDGE

MODEL FM

TO BANBURY

THRUPP BRIDGE

HAMPTON POYLE

MANOR FM

THRUPP

THE JOLLY BOATMAN

THE BELL INN

A 4260

OXFORD CANAL

RIVER CHERWELL

TO OXFORD

Through the back door into Blenheim Park

Maps
Landranger 1:50,000
Sheet 164
Pathfinder 1:25,000
Sheet 1092 (SP 41/51)
Map Reference of Start/
Finish SP412159

How to get there
From the A4095 Witney-
Woodstock road, turn off in
Long Hanborough signposted
to Combe. Just beyond the
railway, turn left past Combe
Halt, and follow the road
uphill through a small wood.
Keep straight on at a junction
at the beginning of the village.
The Cock Inn is on the left and
overlooks the village green.
Combe is served by the
Worths Motor Services route
70 (5 journeys per day
Monday to Saturday; tel. 0608
677322); Combe Halt on the
Oxford-Worcester railway line
is only about half a mile from
the village.

Pub facilities
Cock Inn, Combe
The previous tenant of The
Cock Inn did not supply
meals, so the pub was little
used by walkers; now that the
current landlord and landlady
have rectified this omission,
this friendly local has started
to attract a passing trade. The
stone building overlooking the
green is Grade II listed and

Background to the Walk

Opposite the lake from Blenheim Palace stands a small obelisk, which marks the site of the original royal manor house of Woodstock. Henry II lived here, and installed his mistress Rosamund Clifford in a retreat by a well nearby. The well survives, and is known as Fair Rosamund's Well.

The old manor house survived until 1723. In 1704 John Churchill, Duke of Marlborough, defeated the French at the Battle of Blenheim. In recognition of this military feat, Queen Anne presented the Duke with the royal manor and funds to build a monumental house. The Duke chose the playwright-cum-architect John Vanbrugh and his assistant Nicholas Hawksmoor for this prestigious commission. The obvious choice of architect might have been Sir Christopher Wren (who was Surveyor of the Royal Works at the time), but the Duke had been impressed by Vanbrugh's work at Castle Howard in Yorkshire. The building of Blenheim did not go smoothly, in fact parts of the stable block were never completed. The original working estimate at the start of the project in 1705 was about £40,000. Wren was consulted a little later and suggested a figure nearer £100,000. The expected completion date also slipped (partly because of local quarries proving unable to supply sufficient stone of the required quality, and partly because of the cessation of funding from the Treasury in 1712 when a Tory government came to power). The Marlboroughs funded the works themselves after this. They took up residence in the half-completed building in 1719, but the Duke died only three years later. His widow, who had wanted Wren to

The Cock Inn at Combe

has an open fire which is lit in winter. The pub caters for the village's sports teams on Sundays, and takes a leading role in the annual village feast. The pub also organises a conker competition in the appropriate season. Bar billiards and Aunt Sally are played. Beers are mostly from the Morrell's brewery (this being a Morrell's pub), in addition there is a guest beer available in the winter months. The menu changes quarterly and includes staples such as lasagne, toasted sandwiches, ploughman's and jacket potatoes, as well as steaks, fish dishes and pies. A vegetarian casserole is also available. There is a good-sized garden beyond the car park, and children are welcome at lunchtimes. Opening hours are 1100-1430 and 1800-2300 Monday to Friday (1130-1500 on Saturdays), with the usual restricted opening hours in force on Sundays. Car drivers should note that the gate to the car park is locked outside these hours, so they should park in front of the pub if possible. Parking on the green is forbidden. Tel. 0993 891288.

design the house, fell out with Vanbrugh and Hawksmoor and they were forced to resign. Hawksmoor later returned to the project, but Vanbrugh was refused admission and had to view his creation from outside the park wall in 1725. He died a year later. The house was substantially complete by the early 1730s; the eventual cost is reckoned to have been about £325,000. It has been described as the largest house in England, and covers some seven acres.

The Great Bridge contained numerous chambers, including a boathouse, a bathing house and a pumping engine. It originally spanned a rather insignificant canal between two small lakes. Lancelot 'Capability' Brown was commissioned to landscape the grounds between 1764 and 1774. He dammed the River Glyme and reshaped the valley to form the impressive lake seen today (a small remnant of an earlier dam breaks the surface to form Queen Elizabeth Island north of the bridge). Brown also levelled the so-called military garden to the south of the house and laid it to lawn. Many of the trees in the park follow Brown's original design, and it was Brown who laid out the winding carriage drives between Combe Gate and the lake. It has been claimed that parts of the garden were laid out to echo the pattern of troops at the Battle of Blenheim.

The history of Blenheim did not end here. Winston Churchill was born in the Palace in 1874. Later, just before the First World War, the park was closed after suffragettes threatened vandalism. During the First World War, the park deer (which had been brought from Windsor in 1708) were disposed of, and the library was pressed into service as a hospital ward. The house was closed to visitors in the 1920s, and remained so until the 1950s. During this time tenants included the

Intelligence Services, the British Council and the Ministry of Supply.

Since re-opening, the Palace has become one of the top ten tourist attractions in Britain and receives over 350,000 visitors each year. Modern attractions include a garden centre, an adventure playground and a miniature train. Despite the huge number of visitors to the Palace, the Park is large enough to absorb those who venture into it. This walk traverses the quieter parts of the Park, without neglecting some of the more popular sights.

To the north of the house is the great avenue. This was obviously an integral part of the original park scheme — it forms part of a straight line from Ditchley Gate through the Column of Victory and the centre of the Palace to the distant landmark of Bladon church (where Churchill is buried). There was originally an ellipse partway down the avenue, which may have been intended as the setting for the monument that was eventually built between the avenue and the bridge. This, the Column of Victory, was completed in 1731 and was the home of one of the last breeding pairs of Ravens in the county. Unfortunately one or both were shot in 1847. The avenue was replanted a number of times, most recently (in the 1970s) with limes to replace the elms that had succumbed to Dutch Elm Disease.

To the west of the avenue is Park Farm. This is now the centre for most of the agricultural work that goes on in the northern park, but it once housed a menagerie which included tigers. Until the middle of the last century it was known as the Dog Kennel, probably because the Duke's hounds were quartered there. There was also a horse-racing circuit around the northern end of the park in the 18th century.

Akeman Street, the Roman road, crosses the northern end of the park. By the junction of Akeman Street and the avenue to Ditchley Gate are the remains of Grim's Ditch, an earthwork which forms a semicircle between here and Stonesfield.

The park is one of the premier birdwatching sites in the county, although perhaps not as important as it once was now that flooded gravel pits and reservoirs provide large areas of open water elsewhere. The lake is still the main attraction — large numbers of waterfowl congregate in winter and it is the county's main breeding stronghold for Gadwall (a rather nondescript duck with white flashes on its wings). Great Crested Grebes have bred here since around 1908. Other specialities are Crossbill and Hawfinch, although these are rarely seen, and Redstarts formerly bred in the old oaks (though sadly they do so no longer). A feral flock of Snow Geese is a recent addition to the avifauna of the park. However, the most obvious bird in much of the park is the pheasant — these are bred on a huge scale, and dog-owners should keep their animals on a lead.

Combe village is greatly influenced by its illustrious neighbour. Its name, which suggests a valley site, does not seem to tally with its hilltop position. The explanation is that the village has shifted from its original site near the river Evenlode in the valley to the south. Fragments of roof tiles, slates and part of a 13th-century tomb cover have been found there. The move may have been made to escape the effects of flooding or by the onset of the plague. It did not take place overnight — the two villages seem to have co-existed for some time.

In 1701 the village had ten public houses; this number had dwindled to one by 1774. The total rose again to four in 1820, but nowadays there is only one again (The Cock Inn), and this not on its original site. It was originally on the left-hand side of the lane to the church — this building is now a private dwelling. The church has a rare 15th-century stone pulpit which springs from a corbel formed in the shape of a human head. There are also a number of wall paintings, including a fearsome depiction of the jaws of hell. It seems unlikely that this could ever have been truly terrifying, even in less cynical times — were these the horror films of their day?

Like nearby Stonesfield and Finstock (see Walks 6 and 20), Combe's industries included stone-working and masonry, and the manufacture of gloves. There was also a brickworks at the top of Boltons Lane, operated by the Blenheim Estate around the turn of the century. The Park brought much employment to the villagers; as well as providing domestic and agricultural work, the estate also established a sawmill, where fir trees were brought to be converted into pit props. The sawmill still operates at the bottom of the valley near the railway, which of course also provided much temporary employment when it was constructed through the parish in the 19th century.

Walk 19

Distance: *Allow between three and four hours for this parkland walk of just under six-and-a-half miles.*

Walk straight across the village green from The Cock Inn. In the far corner a road leads off towards the church. By the telephone box beneath the spreading boughs of a large cedar tree, turn right towards the church (passing a village pump — there is another by The Cock Inn). Turn left in the churchyard; the path leads to a stile ingeniously (if rather disrespectfully!) contrived from two headstones. Walk along the top of the sloping recreation ground to a gap in the hedge. Aim slightly left of centre to a break in the next hedge (to the right of an old oak tree). Notice the views to Long Hanborough on the right with the spire of St. Peter and St. Paul, Church Hanborough, behind. Beyond the first hedge the path leads to the near corner of a small wood in a shallow dip, and continues around the right-hand edge. At the corner of the wood, turn left and continue along the outside of the wood. When you reach the end of the wood pass through a hedge and walk across a field to the left of the house opposite, keeping more-or-less parallel with the edge of another wood on the right. This leads to Boltons Lane.

Turn left and walk slightly uphill to a road junction; turn right here into East End. Keep along the lane to Combe Gate, where you turn left through a tall kissing gate by the lodge into Blenheim Park. Just beyond the gate, there is a T-junction. Turn left, and follow the road as it swings right and descends, shallowly at first and then more steeply, through wooded scenery with occasional fields and open areas. Eventually the road reaches the bottom of the valley. Leave it as it swings left and follow the valley down to the right. As you approach the end of an arm of the lake, cross a stile on the left then keep right along the lakeside path.

When you meet the main lake, there is a fine view of the Grand Bridge. Keep above the lake edge as you approach the bridge (you may like to take a detour down a grassy track towards the water to peer over the railings into Fair Rosamund's Well). When you reach the road, turn right to the beginning of the bridge, then double back on another metalled road which leads to the right of the Column of Victory and eventually back to the lakeside (the lake north of the bridge is known as Queen Pool). When you reach the cottage at the end of the lake, keep left up the valley. The road crosses a cattle grid then leads to the left, out of the valley, until it reaches an avenue of small trees. Here turn right and walk along the avenue for nearly three quarters of a mile, passing another cattle grid midway along.

At a third cattle grid, the Oxfordshire Way crosses the avenue level with the farm buildings of Furze Platt on the right. The lodge at Ditchley Gate is visible ahead at the end of the avenue. Notice also the earthworks of Grim's Ditch in the fields on either side. Turn left and follow the Oxfordshire Way through a gate and across a large field. Its line is just as straight as the avenue you have recently left — you are following the line of the Roman road known as Akeman Street. At the end of the field, the path leads down into a belt of woodland at the edge of the park.

The Oxfordshire Way continues over the park wall, but our route turns left and continues through the woods parallel to the wall for about 150 yards. It then turns left, away from the park wall, through the woods and over a wooden bridge. When you reach the edge of the wood, turn right for a short distance, then follow the path out across a further field to reach a belt of trees. Turn right here and walk along the edge of these trees until you meet the track from Park Farm at the end of the wood. Turn right and head to the left of another, smaller, copse then walk along a straggly hedge to the corner of the field. Here a footpath sign marks the path leading down into a valley with wooded sides and a grassy bottom. Walk left down the valley for a short distance, then follow a grassy path up the opposite side. This leads to a track just inside the park wall; turn left for a couple of yards, then turn right to reach some wooden steps over the wall.

Once 'beyond the pale', turn left to the end of a hedge; then turn right (along the far side of the hedge), uphill towards Combe. When the hedge ends (the field boundary marked on the OS Pathfinder map running parallel to the road no longer exists), walk diagonally leftwards to a gate into Park Road. Turn right.

The road leads past several houses and cottages, to the Methodist church. From here admire a splendid village view — the old houses and mature trees of Combe cluster around the church tower in classic fashion, and the village's hilltop position is noticeable. Keep along the edge of the playing field until you reach the cedar tree near the church, where you turn right to reach the end of the walk at the village green.

East End & Stonesfield; to the Roman villa by the Evenlode

Maps

*Landranger 1:50,000
Sheet 164
Pathfinder 1:25,000
Sheet 1091 (SP 21/31)
Map Reference of Start/
Finish SP399144*

How to get there

*From the A4095 between Long
Hanborough and North Leigh,
take the turning to East End
(signposted to the Roman
Villa). Almost immediately,
turn right, still following the
Roman Villa signs. The
Leather Bottel is on the left
shortly after you enter the
village. East End can also be
reached by unclassified roads
from Finstock, Charlbury and
Stonesfield. There is no bus
service to East End, but
Stonesfield is served five times
a day (Mon-Sat) by the
Worths Motor Services route
70 (tel. 0608 677322). Combe
Halt (on the Oxford-
Worcester line) is about 3
miles from East End by road
(or 2 miles by footpath).*

Background to the Walk

This walk has plenty to offer — ancient woodlands, an excavated Roman villa, flowery meadows, disused and overgrown stone quarries, a pretty riverside path, an interesting church, good views and two attractive villages. The Evenlode valley is one of Oxfordshire's finest walking areas, and this is one of the 'best bits'. East End is a village of old cottages strung along the road, which may have been an ancient ridge way. The village once had two pubs, but the New Inn ceased trading (for the second time) in 1958. East End was formerly a quarrying village — the local stone was used for paving slabs, and was also used to build the library of Oriel College, Oxford, in 1788. The remains of the quarries can be seen in the woods between Sturt House (the 18th-century quarry-master's house) and North Leigh Roman Villa.

Iron Age pottery has been found at the quarries, suggesting that the Roman villa was built on the site of an earlier settlement. The villa was a substantial household of the first few centuries AD. It lies just above the River Evenlode, and even today the attractions of the site are obvious — it was close to a road (Akeman Street) with ample supplies of water, wood and building stone and a lovely situation to boot. It was probably occupied by a high-born British family of the Dobunni tribe, rather than by Roman settlers, and seems to have been abandoned in the late 4th or early 5th century. There is some evidence of later occupation by early 'squatters'. The villa was excavated in 1813-16, but the site was soon damaged by souvenir hunters. To prevent further damage, a keeper's cottage (now the ticket

Pub facilities
Leather Bottel, East End
(Pictured left)
This welcoming inn is thought
to have been a public house
since 1721, but the building is
older. In the 19th century it
was the meeting place of the
Bottle club, a Friendly Society
(a prototype building society),
which survived until the
1920s. The pub is said to be
haunted by Ned, the ghost of a
former landlord, who sports a
monocle and a waxed
moustache. There is a sunny
conservatory and a good-sized
garden with swings and an
Aunt Sally pitch. The pub is
open from 1100 till 1500 and
from 1830 to 2330 (Monday
to Saturday), and from 1200
to 1500 on Sundays (the pub
does not open on Sunday
evenings). Food is available
whenever the pub is open. You
can choose from a wide range
of meals, including a
particularly good selection of
vegetarian and vegan dishes.
The most popular starters are
prawn cocktail and garlic
mushrooms, but others are
available; main meals include
steak and kidney pie, duck in
Drambuie, pork and leek
cobbler and bobotie (lamb with
apricots). Ploughman's
lunches, salads and open
sandwiches are available for
those with lighter appetites.
Courage Best bitter, Foster's
and Kronenbourg 1664 lagers
and Woodpecker cider are
served on draught. Children
and dogs are permitted in the
bar as well as the garden.
Patrons are welcome to use the
car park, but are asked not to
consume their own food on the
premises. Bed and breakfast
accommodation is available;
tel. 0993 882174.

office) was built. The Duke of Marlborough gave the site to the Ministry of Works and it is now in the care of English Heritage. It is only open on a few summer Sundays and Bank Holidays, but the site can be overlooked from the footpath. When the ticket office is open, do pay to look round the remains. These include two semicircular baths, but the most impressive of the remains is a fine mosaic (preserved in its own separate building).

Beyond the villa our route crosses the Evenlode by footbridge where Roman travellers along Akeman Street forded the river. It then leads up to the village of Stonesfield.

Stonesfield slates keep the rain out of older buildings for miles around. It is not really slate, but a resistant sandstone. Stone-mining was generally a seasonal occupation, often carried out as a sideline by agricultural workers. Originally the stone was mined in an opencast fashion, but later horizontal and then vertical mines were dug, the deepest reaching down 65 feet. The slatter (who worked all year round) would dampen the stone, then cover it with earth to keep it moist until frost split the stone into slates. The last stone mine at Stonesfield closed around 1910, and the last slate miner died in the 1940s. The remains of stone workings can be seen in the wood above the Roman villa, and again beside the paths between the river and Stonesfield village.

The way up to the village is very unusual for an Oxfordshire path in that there is solid rock underfoot. Surprisingly, the name of the village does not, as might be expected, stem from the slate trade, but is a corruption of 'Stunta's field', or 'fool's field'. The church has a 13th-century chancel arch and some interesting stained glass. Most of the houses in the village are built of stone, naturally, and it is an interesting place to explore. The Oxfordshire Way passes through the village on its 65-mile journey from Bourton-on-the-Water to Henley-on-Thames.

The return journey from Stonesfield to East End crosses the river at the same point as the outward journey, but then takes a lovely path through woods alongside the Evenlode. Take your time along this stretch to enjoy the scenery and to increase your chances of spotting some of the birdlife that abounds in this area — typical common birds to be seen include Treecreeper, Whitethroat and Long-tailed Tit. Kingfisher and Grey Wagtail are also a possibility. Ashford Mill, at the end of this stretch, was once an important river crossing, and Methodist meetings were held here at the crossroads in the 1820s.

A little way on, you pass close to Holly Court Farm. The stream here often dries out and seems much too feeble to have created such a major valley. The mystery is solved when one discovers that this is thought to have been the former course of the River Windrush (which now flows into the Thames at Newbridge — see Walk 5). In Saxon times, the stream was probably known as the Itchen. Even as recently as the 15th century, there was enough water at flood time to damage Holly Court, and there is some evidence that a mill once stood nearby — all rather hard to believe today when looking at the shrunken stream.

The return to the Leather Bottel is through farmland. Prior to enclosure in 1759, this area between Holly Court and East End was known as Over Riding. There are good views to North Leigh — if you scan the horizon carefully, you can pick out the cap of North Leigh's sail-less windmill, built in 1833 and one of the few remaining in the county.

Walk 20

Distance: *Allow three hours for this scenic walk of five miles.*
Note: The walk can be shortened to three-and-three-quarter miles by omitting the loop to Stonesfield village, which includes a steep ascent and descent. Parts of the walk may be muddy or overgrown — boots in winter and long trousers in summer are a must.

Turn left out of the car park of the Leather Bottel, and walk along the main village street. Keep right on to the end of the village then, between Sturt House and the Roman Villa sign, take a footpath on the right into Sturt Copse, signposted to Coombe (*sic*). This path winds through the trees. When it opens out in a grove of mature beech trees, turn left (do not follow the obvious path that descends steeply in front of you). The left-hand path leads shortly to a small stone quarry in a clearing. Look out for the blue flowers of Nettle-leaved Bellflower that grows hereabouts. Beyond the quarries, the path descends quite steeply towards the

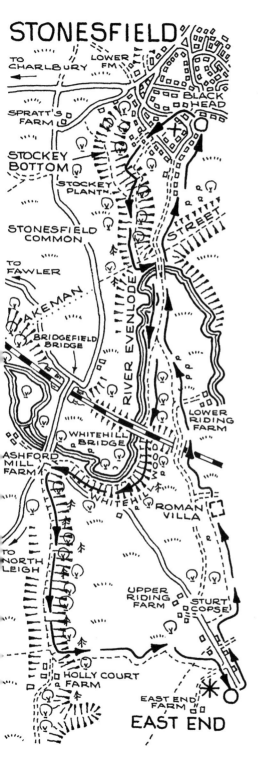

STONESFIELD

Walk 20

KEY

----	FOOTPATH
====	TRACK
≡≡	METALLED ROAD
▬	RAILWAY LINE
〰	RIVER
✝	CHURCH
▫	BUILDING
→	ROUTE OF WALK
O	PUBLIC HOUSE
✳	START POINT OF WALK
⅋⅋⅋⅋	HILL FEATURE
⅏	ROCK CUTTING.

PUB DETAILS

THE START POINT PUBLIC HOUSE IS THE LEATHER BOTTEL AT EAST END.

OTHER PUB FEATURED :- THE BLACK HEAD AT STONESFIELD.

NOTE

THIS MAP IS DIAGRAMMATIC ONLY AND IS NOT TO SCALE.

river. Just before you get to the bottom, the path swings right to avoid a steep bank and a fallen tree then turns left to reach a stile into a field. North Leigh Roman Villa is straight ahead with Stonesfield church visible on the hillside behind. Aim for the left-hand corner of the walled enclosure around the villa and walk along the left-hand side to a stile by the Ticket Office.

Turn left along the grassy track away from the villa, to reach a dusty farm track. Turn right. This track leads downhill to a bridge over the railway. Cross the bridge and keep on along the track. About 100 yards from the railway, the track swings right to Lower Ridings Farm; keep along the grassy field edge straight ahead. The view to the left includes Wilcote House among the trees. The grassy area on the hillside in front of you is Stonesfield Common. The field gate at the bottom of the hill marks the beginning of 'the Stonesfield loop'. If you decide to omit this part of the walk (about one-and-a-quarter miles), find a gap in the hedge to the left, and skip the following paragraph.

Go through the gate and walk across the field in a curve of the Evenlode to a footbridge. This is a popular spot for families to picnic and children to play. Cross the bridge and walk straight up the hill (do not take the Oxfordshire Way which crosses a stile on the right). The path reaches a small quarry face on the right and leads quite steeply uphill, with exposed rock underfoot. The path levels off as it reaches the outskirts of Stonesfield and emerges at the corner of Church Street and Churchfields. Keep straight ahead along Church Street, which curves round to a whitebeam tree in a square by the church. Turn left into the churchyard (notice the worn stone stile at the entrance) and walk by the church to another stone stile at the far end of the churchyard. Turn left, then take a dusty track on the right. This leads between gardens then bends left by a hut with a sign reading Andy's Den. Here, turn right down some steps to a stile. On either side, notice the waste stone from the adjacent quarries. Cross the stile into a flowery meadow and walk down to the bottom of the valley (Stockey Bottom). Cross the stile opposite into the wood and turn left. Follow the path just inside the wood back to the footbridge. Cross back to the south side of the Evenlode and follow the path you walked before to the field gate. Beyond the gate, turn right through a gap in the trees.

The first couple of hundred yards parallel to the river can be rather overgrown, but the path beyond repays any mild discomfort, so do persist. The going becomes rather easier when you reach the wood. The route then leads delightfully alongside the river to the three arches of the railway bridge. Beyond the bridge it continues in a similar vein. Along this stretch, notice where the Stonesfield slate has been weathered out of the riverbank and lies on the bed of the river. When the path finally leaves the river, it passes through a stand of tall aspens, then through a staggered gateway to the road. Turn right and walk along the road for a few yards to a crossroads by Ashford Mill. Turn left (signposted to North Leigh and Witney). About 100 yards along the road, take a bridleway on the left. This path leads between hedges along the bottom of a dry valley. As you approach Holly Court Farm after a quarter of a mile or so, ignore a path leading off on the right.

The excavated remains of North Leigh Roman Villa

The bridleway crosses the bed of a stream, then turns right towards the farm. Level with a derelict and ivy-covered outhouse, take a track on the left that leads uphill through the wood. At the top of the wood, follow a path straight on (although through crops, the line of the path was clear when this walk was last checked). This leads to a gap in the hedge. Beyond this, the path leads straight on across the corner of the field (also well marked). There is a good view of North Leigh on the right from this field.

When you reach the hedge, turn right and walk along the field edge. In the corner of the field, cross a stile on the left under an ash tree. Walk along the field edge then, about 50 yards short of the end of the field, turn right though a gap in the hedge into another field. Walk along the left-hand edge, bypassing an overgrown stile by a further gap in the hedge midway along. Level with a copse on the right, you reach a perpendicular path from North Leigh. Turn left and cross a stile into some fir and fruit trees. Ignore the obvious path straight ahead; instead turn right through the trees. When you reach the corner of a field, aim to the left of the cottage in the far left-hand corner. To the left of the cottage garden is a stile which leads out to the main street in East End. Turn right and make your way back to the Leather Bottel.

A Windrush valley walk from Witney

Walk begins page 126

Maps
Landranger 1:50,000
Sheet 164
Pathfinder 1:25,000
Sheet 1115 (SU 20/30)
Map Reference of Start/
Finish SP355095

How to get there
Witney is reached from
Oxford via the A40 trunk
road, and from Abingdon on
the A415 via Frilford and
Kingston Bagpuize. From the
intersection of these two
roads, follow signs to the
Town Centre, turning right at
the traffic lights on the A415
Ducklington Lane into Station
Lane. Station Lane leads past
an industrial estate on the
right, with the spire of Witney
church overlooking a park on
the left. At the first
roundabout keep straight on
into Witan Way, passing
Farm Mill on the right. At the
second roundabout (by the
Windrush Leisure Centre),
again keep straight on, then
turn immediately left into the
long-stay car park by Waitrose
supermarket. The Butter Cross
is a short walk from the car
park via Langdale Gate. Bus
users can catch any of several
services from Oxford, but
there is no direct service
between Abingdon and
Witney. Witney lost its rail
services in the 1960s.

Background to the Walk

The starting and finishing point of this walk is the rustic Butter Cross in the centre of Witney. Dairy produce, poultry and eggs were sold here during weekly markets, which have taken place, on Thursdays, since 1278 at least. The original cross, which may have supported a statue of the Virgin Mary, was roofed in 1606.

Witney was built on a slight rise above the surrounding flood meadows. An early attempt at improving the productivity of these meadows by digging a drainage ditch is recorded in 1044. This may refer to Em's or Emma's Dyke, encountered during the second half of this walk. Local tradition has it that this stream is named after Queen Emma, who married two kings (Ethelred the Unready and Canute) and bore two more (Hardicanute by her second husband and Edward the Confessor by her first).

Cogges is a small hamlet about half a mile from Witney. The earliest recorded lord of the manor of Cogges was Wadard, a follower of the Norman bishop Odo of Bayeux. Wadard is shown on the Bayeux tapestry directing the plundering of Hastings under the legend HIC EST WADARD ('here is Wadard'). The Manor Farmhouse (which incorporates part of the 13th-century manor) houses the Cogges Manor Farm Museum. This delightful museum shows many facets of country life in times gone by. The farmhouse includes an authentically furnished Edwardian kitchen, drawing and dining room, and the outbuildings and barns house various displays of old-fashioned farming implements and machinery, as well as a variety of old-fashioned breeds of farmyard animal.

Pub facilities
Red Lion Hotel, Witney
(Pictured left)
A few yards down Corn Street from the Butter Cross in the centre of Witney is The Red Lion. This Morrell's house has a comfortable beamed interior and friendly bar staff. The pub is open all day (except Sundays, when normal hours apply). Closing time is 2300 on Tuesdays and Wednesdays, but on Mondays, Thursdays, Fridays and Saturdays the pub stays open late and live music is performed in the Barn, an extra bar behind the main pub. Children are not allowed in the main bar, but for warmer weather there is a small courtyard between the main building and the Barn, and there are also plans to open the Barn at lunchtimes as a Family Room. Food is good, with a wide menu including steaks, vegetarian dishes and sandwiches. The latter are something of a speciality. A daily special is also available every day except Sunday. Beers include Morrell's Best and Graduate, plus a monthly guest beer and the usual range of lagers and ciders. The Lounge Bar is decorated with modern prints, and a curiosity of the Public Bar is the round pool table; there is also a dart board. Tel. 0993 703149.

Witney is famous for its blankets, which are soft and of good quality; so much so that even Yorkshire firms sometimes sold their products as 'Witney blankets'. A court case in 1908 put a stop to that, but the name was so important that some northern manufacturers opened finishing plants in Witney so that they could continue to use it. The reasons for the emergence of Witney as a centre of blanket-making are fairly clear: the town had a good local supply of wool, and the Windrush water was said to be particularly suitable (Dr. Plot, the 17th-century historian described: 'the Nitrous Windrush, so well impregnated with that abstersive salt, that no flow yields Blanketing so notoriously white as is made at Witney'.) Less obviously perhaps, clean air was also an advantage, as blankets were often dried outside on frames called 'tenters' (hence the phrase 'on tenter-hooks').

The village of Ducklington lives up to its attractive name only in certain parts; the grouping of church, school, pub, village green and pond is particularly pretty. A highlight of the Ducklington year is when the rare Snakeshead Fritillary blooms in a water-meadow near the route of this walk. The village holds a 'Fritillary Sunday' (usually on the first Sunday in May) when the plants can be viewed, the church is open to visitors and teas are served in the village hall. The flower features in two places inside the church: in a stained glass window and on the altar cloth.

*Ducklington's two thatched pubs, the **Bell** and the **Strickland Arms**, are conveniently placed for a mid-walk drink. The former lies on the village green close to the church; the latter is in Witney Road and serves several real ales and a wide selection of food.*

The highlight of the return journey is Witney Parish Church which, like that at Cogges, is dedicated to St. Mary. The impressive Early English steeple rises to 150 feet and is thought to have been modelled on that of Bayeux Cathedral in Normandy. A touching feature is a little carved monkey part way up; tradition has it that this is a sad memorial to a young monkey which escaped from a cruel fairground entertainer at Witney Feast and climbed the steeple, but lost its grip and fell to its death.

In the garden of Mount House, to the east of the church, are the excavated remains of Witney Palace. These remains, described as 'some of the most impressive new medieval discoveries in England this century', belong to a great house built in the early 12th century for the Bishop of Winchester, Henry of Blois. Bishop Henry's brother Stephen was crowned king of England in 1135. The remains were only discovered in 1984 and are still being excavated; currently the site is not generally open to the public, but there are plans to open it in due course.

Henry Box School, off Church Green, was founded in 1660, and the original schoolhouse is still in use (though surrounded by more recent buildings). Near the school entrance are the 'bread and beef' cottages. These were originally almshouses, but were later let for rent; the rent was used to feed the poor, hence the nickname.

Walk 21

Distance: *Allow about 2 hours for this town, village and riverside walk of about three-and-a-quarter miles.*

From the Butter Cross, walk down the left-hand side of Langdale Gate. A side path leads by the car park to a roundabout by the Windrush Leisure Centre. Cross Witan Way to the left of the roundabout, and follow the combined footpath and cycleway between the Witney Community Centre and an electricity substation. This leads very shortly to Langel Bridge over the first strand of the River Windrush. A short, worthwhile there-and-back diversion continues straight on, over the other stream, to Cogges and the Farm Museum. Returning to Langel Bridge, turn left (downstream) along the eastern bank. Cross a side ditch (this may involve a short jump in very wet weather!) and continue along the river. Shortly afterwards the two strands of the river come close together, and some of the animal inhabitants of the Farm Museum may be seen in the fields to the left.

A little further on, the path skirts Farm Mill. This stands on the site of one of the two mills mentioned under 'Witenie' in Domesday. Keep left past some allotments to a metal field gate and kissing gate. Aim slightly right, away from the left-hand stream. The path leads under the right-hand line of electricity wires to rejoin the right-hand stream, then crosses two dismantled railways. The first is the former branch line to Witney; the second is the extension to Lechlade and Fairford. The last train travelled the line in 1970, but both bridges over the Windrush are still in place. Pass through a wooden gate and follow an obvious path straight ahead towards the A40. In the far right-hand corner of the field, the path leads under the main road alongside the river. (In very wet weather, the path may be under water;

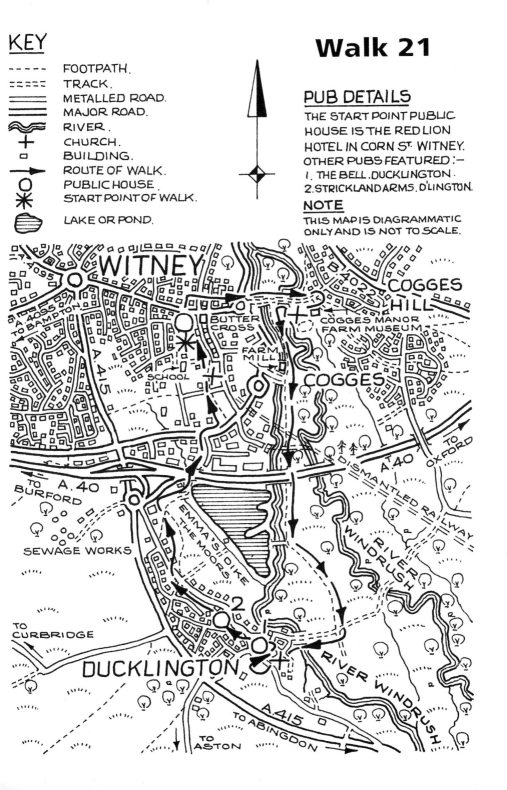

in this situation, unless you fancy the unofficial and highly dangerous crossing of the A40, you are advised to turn back.)

Beyond the bridge, the path returns to the field and continues alongside the river, with views to a lake on the right. A bridge leads over the river on the right to the lakeside; ignore it and follow the river as it swings left to a stile into a further field. Walk straight across to a gate by a projecting corner of the opposite hedge. Here a stile gives access to a track along the field edge. Just beyond the end of the right-hand field, you reach a crossroads; turn right. This track leads shortly to a bridge over the river at the outskirts of Ducklington. Cross and walk on into the village, keeping left past the extended cemetery towards the church. Walk on around the churchyard to visit the Bell pub and to admire the view of the pond, green and church. Then retrace your steps to the rear of the church.

Here turn left and walk along Church Street. Pass The Square on the right to return to the main village street (Witney Road) passing some tumbledown farm buildings on the right just before the junction. Turn right along Witney Road, passing Manor Farm, and the entrances to Pound Close and Tristram Road, on the left. Beyond the Strickland Arms, Ducklington Baptist Church is passed on the right-hand side. When Curbridge Road meets Witney Road by a children's play area, turn right down a path at the end of a row of modern houses (*not* along the concrete track). Behind the houses, a wooden footpath sign indicates the way left along the back of the gardens. At the end of the row, the path swings right. This area was once allotment gardens, but is now overgrown; the path however is metalled and easy to follow. At the end of this section, there is a footbridge with a stile at either end; this leads into an attractive water meadow. The path then leads back towards Witney along a low causeway with a couple of plank bridges. At the end of the water meadow, the path swings right to a further footbridge (ignore the stile over the fence just before the bridge). Once over the footbridge, the path leads to the right, with allotments on the left. When you reach Emma's Dyke turn left, then cross to the other bank with the lake in front of you. Turn left along the stream, passing (but not crossing) another footbridge to follow the stream under the A40.

On emerging from the tunnel the path swings right and enters the least attractive section of the walk, through the Station Lane Industrial Estate. When you reach the main road (Station Lane), cross at the traffic island and turn right. Shortly afterwards, turn left and follow a fine avenue of lime trees across The Leys towards the church. Pass along Church Walk behind the church to emerge in Church Green. The last section of the walk leads pleasantly across the green back to the Butter Cross.

Note: If you have any comments or suggestions (preferably borne from experience) as to how we can improve the information in this book write to us at Ensign Publications, 2 Redcar Street, Southampton SO15 5LL

We will be pleased to supply a list of the other books in this series.